OPPOSING
VIEWPOINTS®
SERIES

P9-DOE-045

Work and Family

DISCARD

Other Books of Related Interest:

Opposing Viewpoints Series:

Child Custody
Male and Female Roles
Unemployment

At Issue Series:

Child Labor and Sweatshops
Does Outsourcing Harm America?
Foster Care

Current Controversies Series:

Jobs in America
Consumer Debt

> "Congress shall make no law ... abridging the freedom of speech, or of the press."

First Amendment to the US Constitution

The basic foundation of our democracy is the First Amendment guarantee of freedom of expression. The Opposing Viewpoints Series is dedicated to the concept of this basic freedom and the idea that it is more important to practice it than to enshrine it.

OPPOSING VIEWPOINTS® SERIES

Work and Family

Mitchell Young, Book Editor

GREENHAVEN PRESS
A part of Gale, Cengage Learning

GALE
CENGAGE Learning·

Detroit • New York • San Francisco • New Haven, Conn • Waterville, Maine • London

Elizabeth Des Chenes, *Managing Editor*

© 2012 Greenhaven Press, a part of Gale, Cengage Learning

Gale and Greenhaven Press are registered trademarks used herein under license.

For more information, contact:
Greenhaven Press
27500 Drake Rd.
Farmington Hills, MI 48331-3535
Or you can visit our Internet site at gale.cengage.com.

For product information and technology assistance, contact us at:

Gale Customer Support, 1-800-877-4253.
For permission to use material from this text or product, submit all requests online at www.cengage.com/permissions.

Further permissions questions can be emailed to permissionrequest@cengage.com.

Articles in Greenhaven Press anthologies are often edited for length to meet page requirements. In addition, original titles of these works are changed to clearly present the main thesis and to explicitly indicate the author's opinion. Every effort is made to ensure that Greenhaven Press accurately reflects the original intent of the authors. Every effort has been made to trace the owners of copyrighted material.

Cover image © iofoto/Shutterstock.com.

LIBRARY OF CONGRESS CATALOGING-IN-PUBLICATION DATA

Work and family / Mitchell Young, book editor.
     p. cm. -- (Opposing viewpoints)
    Includes bibliographical references and index.
    ISBN 978-0-7377-5769-9 (hardcover) -- ISBN 978-0-7377-5770-5 (pbk.)
1. Work and family. I. Young, Mitchell.
    HD4904.25.W6624 2012
    306.3'6--dc23

                    2011045785

Printed in the United States of America
1 2 3 4 5 6 7 16 15 14 13 12

Contents

Chapter 3: How Do Government Policies Affect the Work-Family Balance?

Chapter 4. How Does Lack of Work Affect Families?

Why Consider Opposing Viewpoints?

> *"The only way in which a human being can make some approach to knowing the whole of a subject is by hearing what can be said about it by persons of every variety of opinion and studying all modes in which it can be looked at by every character of mind. No wise man ever acquired his wisdom in any mode but this."*
>
> *John Stuart Mill*

In our media-intensive culture it is not difficult to find differing opinions. Thousands of newspapers and magazines and dozens of radio and television talk shows resound with differing points of view. The difficulty lies in deciding which opinion to agree with and which "experts" seem the most credible. The more inundated we become with differing opinions and claims, the more essential it is to hone critical reading and thinking skills to evaluate these ideas. Opposing Viewpoints books address this problem directly by presenting stimulating debates that can be used to enhance and teach these skills. The varied opinions contained in each book examine many different aspects of a single issue. While examining these conveniently edited opposing views, readers can develop critical thinking skills such as the ability to compare and contrast authors' credibility, facts, argumentation styles, use of persuasive techniques, and other stylistic tools. In short, the Opposing Viewpoints Series is an ideal way to attain the higher-level thinking and reading skills so essential in a culture of diverse and contradictory opinions.

In addition to providing a tool for critical thinking, Opposing Viewpoints books challenge readers to question their own strongly held opinions and assumptions. Most people form their opinions on the basis of upbringing, peer pressure, and personal, cultural, or professional bias. By reading carefully balanced opposing views, readers must directly confront new ideas as well as the opinions of those with whom they disagree. This is not to argue simplistically that everyone who reads opposing views will—or should—change his or her opinion. Instead, the series enhances readers' understanding of their own views by encouraging confrontation with opposing ideas. Careful examination of others' views can lead to the readers' understanding of the logical inconsistencies in their own opinions, perspective on why they hold an opinion, and the consideration of the possibility that their opinion requires further evaluation.

Evaluating Other Opinions

To ensure that this type of examination occurs, Opposing Viewpoints books present all types of opinions. Prominent spokespeople on different sides of each issue as well as well-known professionals from many disciplines challenge the reader. An additional goal of the series is to provide a forum for other, less known, or even unpopular viewpoints. The opinion of an ordinary person who has had to make the decision to cut off life support from a terminally ill relative, for example, may be just as valuable and provide just as much insight as a medical ethicist's professional opinion. The editors have two additional purposes in including these less known views. One, the editors encourage readers to respect others' opinions—even when not enhanced by professional credibility. It is only by reading or listening to and objectively evaluating others' ideas that one can determine whether they are worthy of consideration. Two, the inclusion of such viewpoints encourages the important critical thinking skill of objectively evaluating an author's credentials and bias. This evaluation will illuminate an author's reasons for taking a particular stance on an issue and will aid in readers' evaluation of the author's ideas.

It is our hope that these books will give readers a deeper understanding of the issues debated and an appreciation of the complexity of even seemingly simple issues when good and honest people disagree. This awareness is particularly important in a democratic society such as ours in which people enter into public debate to determine the common good. Those with whom one disagrees should not be regarded as enemies but rather as people whose views deserve careful examination and may shed light on one's own.

Thomas Jefferson once said that "difference of opinion leads to inquiry, and inquiry to truth." Jefferson, a broadly educated man, argued that "if a nation expects to be ignorant and free . . . it expects what never was and never will be." As individuals and as a nation, it is imperative that we consider the opinions of others and examine them with skill and discernment. The Opposing Viewpoints Series is intended to help readers achieve this goal.

David L. Bender and Bruno Leone,
Founders

Introduction

> *"Families are the cornerstone of
> society. . . . They are a crucial
> engine of solidarity, redistributing
> resources (cash, in-kind or time)
> among individuals, households and
> generations. They provide protection
> and insurance against hardship.
> Families offer identity, love, care and
> development to their members and
> form the core of many social networks."*
>
>

*Organization for Economic
Cooperation and Development
(OECD), "Doing Better for
Families," OECD Publishing, 2011.
www.oecd-ilibrary.org.*
>

The family is a refuge for the individual in a world of giant corporations and impersonal bureaucracies—a place of long lasting relationships in a highly mobile, ever-changing world. In part because families act as shelters from outside pressures, they are largely seen as outside the purview of government policy. But families are important to all of society; decisions made within a single household may have barely perceptible effects on a nation, but changes in patterns of family life have repercussions beyond the walls of the family home. Individual decisions about whether and when to marry, and couples' decisions whether and how many children to raise have an impact on the entire society. In much of the industrialized world, fewer people are marrying and couples are deciding to have fewer (or no) children. This is, in part, a response to the difficulty of balancing career and familial requirements. But shrinking populations pose a risk to economies, and some governments are devising policies to help family formation.

The entry of large numbers of women into the workforce has been blamed for the "birth dearth." In 1983 then prime minister Lee Kuan Yew of Singapore exclaimed, "You just can't be doing a full-time, heavy job like that of a doctor or engineer and run a home and bring up children." But even he recognized that the days of most women remaining at home were over, noting that women "will not stand" for being relegated to the role of mother and in any case working women were "too important a factor in the economy."

Still, Singapore and other developed countries have tried to do something about the decline in numbers of children being born, with a goal of reaching "replacement rate" fertility of an average of 2.1 children for each woman over her lifetime. There are two main weapons governments use in their battle to avoid aging and declining populations: offering families tax credits or other monetary incentives for the birth of children and adopting work-family reconciliation policies—policies for child-care and leave that enable parents to look after their young children. It is the second category of policies that most directly affects how mothers and fathers choose to reconcile their work obligations with those of raising children.

The Nordic countries have been pioneers in easing the burden of both parenting and working. According to data from the Organization for Economic Cooperation and Development (OECD), Finland, Sweden, Denmark and Norway all have long-established programs offering generous leave benefits for mothers who have just given birth. Sweden offers the longest period of benefits at sixty-two weeks, though it awards the new mother only about two-thirds of her working wages. Denmark offers full (100 percent) replacement of wages, though for a relatively short (for Scandinavia) thirty weeks. In contrast Mediterranean countries such as Spain, Italy, and Greece have only relatively recently mandated paid maternity leave, and the benefits are less generous than those in Northern Europe.

At first glance it appears that the Nordic policies have worked. For women born between 1945 and 1963, most Scandinavian countries experienced only small declines in the total number of children born per woman, and Finland even posted an increase. In contrast, women born in the late 1950s and early 1960s in Greece, Spain, and Italy had far fewer children than their counterparts a generation earlier. By the year 2000 the stereotypical large Southern European family was vanishing, while the modest-sized Northern European family remained stable. The consequences of this dramatic change are being felt now; for example, a financial crisis in Greece is being fueled in part by relatively few younger workers paying for the retirement benefits of the larger older generation.

The Nordic countries' achievement in maintaining relatively high levels of fertility is more impressive because they also have maintained high levels of female employment. Despite bearing more children, Scandinavian women are more likely to be in the workforce than their Southern European sisters. This paradox may be due to Northern European policies, both governmental and corporate, to ease mothers' transition out of and back into the workforce. For example, professional and technical level part-time work is more available in Sweden than in Italy; Swedish mothers thus have more options to balance family with career than their Italian counterparts have. Governments encourage these policies, but many private firms in Northern Europe report they would offer various work schedule options even without government incentives as workplace flexibility helps them retain valuable employees.

In economically advanced countries, social scientists, government bureaucrats, and corporate human resources specialists are still analyzing data in an effort to create optimal work-life policies, which will ease the path for those women and men who wish to raise the next generation. The comparison between

Scandinavia and the Mediterranean countries seems to offer some preliminary lessons. The main one is that, as Lee Kuan Yew said of Singapore, there is no going back to the days of the strictly stay-at-home mom. Women want to have careers outside the home. The Nordic countries, through programs encouraging flexible work schedules as well as generous maternity benefits, have managed to ease the burdens that parenthood imposes on workers and, for that reason, seem to have avoided drastic declines in family size. In contrast in Southern Europe where maternity benefits are less well established and part-time work less available, people appear to have chosen work over reproduction, a situation that may lead to grave economic and social consequences in the near future.

Regardless of government and corporate policies, most choices men and women make about marriage and children focus on their own desires with regard to career and family. *Opposing Viewpoints: Work and Family* addresses important questions about how individuals and society as a whole strike a balance between work and family in the following chapters: How Do Women Balance Work and Family?, How Do Men Balance Work and Family?, How Do Government Policies Affect the Work-Family Balance?, and How Does Lack of Work Affect Families? There is no doubt that with difficult times in the world economy, the threat of shrinking populations, and continuing reassessment of gender roles, these questions will continue to be debated long into the future.

CHAPTER 1

How Do Women Balance Work and Family?

Chapter Preface

According to the United States Department of Labor, the percentage of women who are in the civilian workforce increased from 43 percent to 59 percent between 1970 and 2009. Despite the clear majority of women working outside the home, they are still seen as the primary caregivers for children. A 2004 study by the New America Foundation reported that 70 percent of women claimed they took more responsibility for routine child care than did their male partners. When it comes to balancing the demands of work and family, the data show that women have a harder task in front of them than men.

With women providing the bulk of care for children, it is not surprising to see an abundance of newspaper and magazine articles about mothers' difficulties managing home and career. Much of this discussion has taken place from a professional, upper-middle-class perspective. The debate over whether women can "have it all"—where "all" means a high-flying career and an ideal family—is largely a discussion among well-off Americans. But for the majority of American mothers, work is not optional. Their primary goal is not making it to the executive suite, but simply paying the bills. For the working woman who works out of necessity, the conflict between family and employment may be more severe than for other, more financially secure women.

One illustration of the bind middle- and working-class mothers face is the prevalence of women in part-time work. Twenty-five percent of women work part time versus eleven percent of men. Some mothers may choose less than full-time employment in order to accommodate societal expectations that they care for their children. According to a study by the Employment Foundation, of men who worked part time, only 12 percent did so because of childcare and family-related issues. The same figure for women part-time workers was 45 percent. Clearly part-time employment offers the benefit of more flexibility to tailor work schedules around family needs. On the down side, less-than-full time workers tend to receive lower wages, are much less likely to receive health insurance or other nonwage benefits, and are at greater risk of layoffs. All of this adds up to a precarious financial position for women who must work part time to make ends meet.

The following viewpoints reflect the work-family balance dilemmas faced by the more affluent women of society. There is no doubt these women face real problems in balancing their careers with the needs of their families. It is worth remembering, however, that for many women the question is not "having it all," but having enough—enough money to pay the bills and enough time to properly care for their children.

> *"There's no need to throw the whole question of work overboard—maybe you can scale back a bit or change jobs."*

Ambitious Women Can Strike a Balance Between Work and Family

India Knight

In the following viewpoint, British journalist and author India Knight acknowledges that women must make sacrifices if they want both a career and a family. She argues, however, that compromising in both areas of life—being less than perfect in housework and cooking as well as working at a less demanding job—is worth it. She believes that giving up a career entirely can lead to financial insecurity and less emotional satisfaction. Women who do combine family with work are happier as individuals, according to Knight, and that makes for a more successful marriage.

As you read, consider the following questions:

1. According to the survey Knight quotes, what attributes in a woman do men value?

2. According to the same survey, what are women looking for in a man?

3. Instead of worrying about the either/or of family versus work, what question does Knight suggest people should ask?

To any woman out there who still wants to "have it all": take a look at Sarah Palin, named on Friday as [2008 Republican presidential nominee] John McCain's running mate. Palin, 44, is the governor of Alaska. She comes from a family of outdoor enthusiasts: as a child, she and her father would get up at 3 AM to hunt moose, a pursuit she still enjoys (she likes to eat moose-burgers, too). At school, Sarah played basketball so enthusiastically—despite once having a fractured ankle—that she was nicknamed "Barracuda".

She was head of the school Fellowship of Christian Athletes and would lead the team in prayer before matches. Palin is a lifetime member of the National Rifle Association and opposes same-sex marriage.

A committed pro-lifer, she has five children. They are called Track (he's in the army), Bristol, Willow, Piper and Trig. When Trig was born with Down syndrome earlier this year [2008], Palin was back at her desk within three days. And now she's the Republican vice-presidential candidate. She's got it all. And she is my idea of a complete nightmare. You do also slightly wonder what the American public, who found Hillary Clinton so off-puttingly high achieving, will make of her.

Shades of Gray

What is odd about the eternal debate on working versus stay-at-home mothers and about the vexed question of what women want is that the choices offered are so starkly black and white when, as we all know, the real world—apart from Palin's—is largely made up of shades of grey.

Yet another survey last week found that the attributes most valued in a partner were straight out of the 1950s: men wanted someone who would: 1) "take care of the home", 2) cook, 3) clean and 4) be a good parent. Women wanted a retrosexual [an old-fashioned man] who had "financial stability" and was, er, good at gardening. Do people seriously walk around thinking: "Tall, dark and handsome, on the rich side, amazingly skilled when it comes to perennials"? Apparently so. (No mention was made of sex, which is strange since most marriages flounder from sexual boredom or incompatibility.)

We may not all discount otherwise attractive men because their plant-caring skills are disappointing, but the list of men's female requisites has become depressingly familiar. They want a clean fragrant home, a clean fragrant wife, a fragrant dinner on the table and a couple of clean fragrant sprogs [children]. Fair enough—who doesn't, women included? The question isn't whether these desires are absurd or retrograde, but why it is automatically assumed that as a woman you can't fulfill them if you are also employed. Why?

The Advantages of Working

Let's take fragrance. Working women win hands down: they're far better dressed, pulled together in a way that remains elusive for some of us: I know that working from home with one eye on the children (no make-up, unappealing tracksuit bottoms, ancient T-shirt, huge socks, slightly dog-smelling bobbly cardigan) isn't a devastatingly good look and that women who go out to work tend to score rather more points on the sartorial front: they own clothes that aren't elasticated, for a start.

Clean fragrant home? Well yes, thanks to the cleaning lady, if you can afford one and it becomes a great deal easier to afford if you have two salaries coming in. Does it matter whether your wife cleans or whether she pays someone else to do it?

Dinner on the table? Well yes, we all have to eat but again, why is there an assumption that working women can't cook or

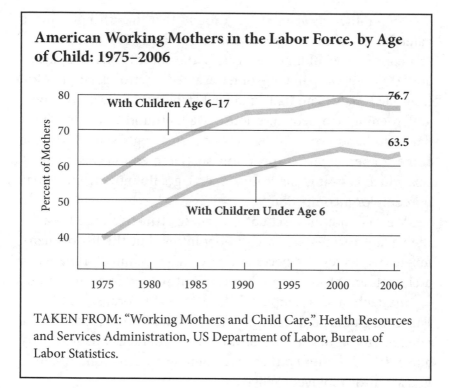

American Working Mothers in the Labor Force, by Age of Child: 1975–2006

With Children Age 6–17 ... 76.7

With Children Under Age 6 ... 63.5

Percent of Mothers

80 70 60 50 40

1975 1980 1985 1990 1995 2000 2006

TAKEN FROM: "Working Mothers and Child Care," Health Resources and Services Administration, US Department of Labor, Bureau of Labor Statistics.

are programmed to produce inferior food? They may not spend the afternoon making pastry, but most people can knock up dinner regardless of whether they've spent the day looking after children or looking after contracts. As for being a good parent—which comes fourth, you will notice, on the list of requirements—well, you're either a good parent or you're not: I don't think having a job disqualifies you.

Still on this subject, Fiona Phillips, 47, the [British] breakfast television presenter, announced last week that she was quitting her job at GMTV [English television show "Good Morning TV"] after nearly 16 years. "I love the job but I've got other responsibilities—the children, a home life and an elderly dad who needs me—and I've recognised that I can't have it all," she said. Phillips's children are aged nine and six and it's easy to see that the 4 AM start is tricky to build into family life.

Having Quite a Lot

What I hope Phillips and the thousands of other women in her position trying to balance work and family life realise is that while you can't have it all, you can certainly make a good fist of having quite a lot. This, surely, is what we should be concentrating on: not the either/or debate that has plagued the question of working mothers for so long, but the question of how much we can grab without causing too much collateral damage.

There's no need to throw the whole question of work overboard—maybe you can scale back a bit or change jobs. But surveys such as this one increasingly show that women are chucking out the baby, as it were, with the bath water. It seems an awful shame. The trick is to find—or invent—a balance, to make it work for you and to be unapologetic about it.

Phillips, for instance, has found getting up in the middle of the night impossible to reconcile with her domestic life—and who would blame her? She has, she says, every intention of continuing to work in television, which is as it should be, since working in television is what she does.

For many people, finding that balance is an exhausting, sometimes demoralising, process not helped by family-hostile employers or organisations—but it can, and should, be attempted. Forget about the things men allegedly look for in a spouse. They're not quite as important as the things women want for themselves, such as financial security, professional success, emotional satisfaction and healthy relationships with spouse and children.

These things matter more than being good at making cottage pie or having perfectly applied lipstick. Or hunting moose, for that matter. And, despite what the silly survey suggests, these things are crucial in terms of relationships between the sexes. Because men always run screaming—guaranteed—from an unhappy woman, trailing her misery and resentment behind her like a cloak. Do what makes you happy.

> "Husbands tried to be helpful, to lighten
> the load, but even the most willing
> among them were simply not around
> enough for their efforts to make much
> of a contribution."

Pressure from Husbands Leads Women to Sacrifice Career for Family

Pamela Stone

Pamela Stone's most recent work, Opting Out?: Why Women Really Quit Careers and Head Home, *is the source of the following viewpoint. Stone investigates why several relatively wealthy former career women decided to stay at home to raise their children. Basing her analysis on in-depth interviews with the women, Stone argues that husbands have a major influence on women's decision to "opt-out" of their careers. Having a husband whose salary enables the wife to stay at home is a huge factor. But beyond that, according to Stone, there is a more subtle pressure being exerted by the men in these relationships. While they are verbally supportive of their wives' choices, they do not volunteer to assume the child-rearing role. By putting the man's career first, consciously or not, couples devalue the woman's career. Stone is a professor of sociology at the City Univer-*

sity of New York. In addition to publishing books and scholarly articles, she has discussed her work frequently on television and radio.

As you read, consider the following questions:

1. How do economists explain the phenomenon of women in wealthier couples giving up high-powered careers to stay at home with children?
2. In what way does the traditional, male-oriented professional career path conflict with women's biology, according to this author?
3. How does men's rhetoric about careers and childcare conflict with their behavior, at least as far as the couples profiled in the viewpoint are concerned?

Husbands appeared to exercise a little remarked-on but powerful and benevolent presence in women's thinking. Most obviously, husbands' earnings were clearly the necessary precondition that made it possible for them to stay home. Women were grateful for having this option whether they acknowledged it explicitly or not. The taken-for-granted nature of this arrangement was to some extent a reflection of their up-bringing in traditional families; to them it was the status quo. It was also a reflection of the general success these women had enjoyed in other aspects of their lives. High-achieving themselves, women just assumed that their husbands (whom they had often met at school, when they were seen to have similarly good prospects and high potential) would do well too.

Wealth Means Choice

Patricia Lambert, the legislative prodigy turned marketing executive, was one of the few women to openly acknowledge her husband's role in making it possible for her to stay home:

> He was making enough money that we didn't have to have my income, which, by the way, I want to just say this underlies

my whole decision making, and we were very lucky that we
didn't have to, either because of our choice of lifestyle or his
absolute income. Early on our choices of lifestyle, and later
on his absolute income, have given us this flexibility, which I
completely—I don't want to not be grateful and aware of that.
We really had a choice, and most women don't. And I see that
in my sister-in-law who is a nurse.

Other women acknowledged their husband's contribution
obliquely, commenting, as Meg Romano did, on their good for-
tune or luck in being able to stay home: "I think that from my
perspective I feel incredibly lucky. I know that I'm incredibly
lucky to be able to be home. Not all women have that option."

For economists, affluent wives' staying home is easily explained (if not dismissed) as a "wealth effect," made possible
by the growing concentration of wealth among couples such as
these dual professionals. Over time, perhaps, growing wealth at
the top could explain such a trend, but at any one point in time
many wives of high-earning men do pursue careers (for the last
few decades, the majority, in fact). In addition, research shows
that women's decision making about careers—and the fundamental question of whether or not to pursue them—is more and
more a function of what *they* bring to the table in terms of education, training, commitment, interest, and prospective earnings,
rather than what husbands provide by way of income. There was
earnings variation among the husbands (who ranged from small
business owners, to professionals such as lawyers and doctors,
to corporate CEOs) of the women in this study, but most made
more than ample livings. As a result, few women cited the pinch
of lost earnings as a factor in their deliberations about quitting.
Although most of these couples were not wealthy, they were
clearly comfortable, making it possible for women to exercise
discretion in assessing their options. While husbands' income
was certainly a necessary condition of their quitting (as Patricia's
comment makes clear), it was not a sufficient one. Other fac-

tors figured in, children primary among them as we have already seen. Moreover, even husbands' influence went beyond earning power. Their high earnings made it unnecessary for these women to work and possible for them to quit, but husband's earnings are not *why* they quit. In other words, *how much* husbands earned enabled their wives to quit; *how* they earned it and the circumstances of their employment gave wives a reason to do so.

Career Versus Biology

Common knowledge has it that women and men see traffic lights differently. When the light changes to yellow, women treat it as a caution to put on the brakes, men as a signal to floor it. With regard to their careers, children and family are the yellow light; women slow down and men speed up. The so-called "clockwork of male careers" explains some of this gender difference. The trajectories of the professions, historically male-dominated, are structured according to the rhythms and timing of men's lives. The period of career establishment and growth corresponds to what are for women the prime childbearing and rearing years. This "clockwork" pressure is external—the clash of culturally constructed careers with the biology of reproduction. But the yellow light phenomenon is also the result of internal pressures within marriage, a reflection of the respective power that each party brings to the table as they negotiate to accommodate careers and children.

These women, in common with virtually all women, even other professionals, shouldered the vast majority of the responsibilities of caring for children and parents (including recruiting and supervising paid caregivers) and of overseeing the myriad duties of running a household. Husbands played a role in women's decisions, not by virtue of "king of the castle" demands they made for their own care and feeding, nor by imposing strict housekeeping standards. Rather, husbands' primary influence was felt through what work-family scholars call "crossover," by which the demands of husbands' careers cross over and affect their wives'. Most of these men, by the way, judging from the women's narratives, were neither unfeeling louts nor exploitive cads. In fact, women repeatedly described their husbands as "good fathers." Husbands tried to be helpful, to lighten the load, but even the most willing among them were simply not around enough for their efforts to make much of a contribution. This combination of husbands' unavailability, inability, and/or unwillingness (there were no cases of outright refusal) to shoulder significant portions of caregiving and family responsibilities weighed heavily on women's decisions to quit, because it often fell to them to pick up the pieces and the slack. Their efforts to do so resulted in significant and cumulative disadvantages to their careers relative to their husbands' which further served to undermine their relatively more equal position as part of a two-professional couple and to weaken their connection to their own careers in a self-perpetuating cycle that led to quitting.

Helena Norton, an educational administrator who characterized her husband as a "workaholic," described poignantly a scenario that many others took for granted and which illustrates a pattern typical of many of these women's lives:

> He was leaving early mornings; 6:00 or 6:30 before anyone was up, and then he was coming home late at night. So I felt this real emptiness, getting up in the morning to, not necessarily an empty house, because my children were there, but I did, I felt empty, and then going to bed, and he wasn't there.

Because their own jobs often made similar demands, women could anticipate and empathize with their husbands' grueling routines. Here, Rachel Berman, a Wall Street trader, reflects on how her husband's new position in a field akin to her own influenced her decision to stay home:

> My husband had taken a job three months earlier with another investment bank, and we knew his life was going to go to hell,

because he was in the mergers and acquisitions department of [a high-profile firm that] was in the paper today. He was working with those men. So we knew that his life would be non-stop travel . . . and we decided that somebody should be home to be more attentive to the kids, because now we had a second child.

These couples could delegate child care and housekeeping to paid help (overseen by wives). As a result, the more mundane stresses associated with juggling two careers and kids were not major themes in their reasons for quitting. Their husbands' demanding careers *did* put a great deal of pressure on women to do it all, but the effect of husbands' absence was felt in more fundamental ways that had do with the construction of a family unit and the creation of a [nurturing] and supportive environment for the children. Women were less focused on their husbands' inability to perform the day-to-day tasks of grocery shopping, cooking, and cleaning; they talked little about "chore wars." Stephanie Spano's husband's non-stop routine was not atypical. Between his schedule and hers working four days a week as a management consultant, it was hard to find time for family life:

> He's got a very flexible job in that he owns his own company. He makes his own hours. That said, he works seven days a week. He owns a real estate company, and people want to see homes on Saturday and Sunday. . . . We had precious little family time, in part because, you know, here I am working like thirty hours. I have one day off, Friday, but my husband's not home Saturday and Sunday either.

Leah Evans, a health care administrator married to a high-level corporate executive, expressed the dilemma facing couples with (typically two) children and two careers: "*Somebody's* got to be there."

Permission Granted

As women struggled to juggle kids and careers, largely on their own, and as they deliberated about whether or not to quit, they were influenced by their husbands' attitudes towards their careers and towards the prospect of their giving them up. Some husbands were genuinely supportive of whatever decision a woman wanted to make. Nan Driscoll, who was an editor-in-chief of a publishing company, had such a husband, one she described as "terrifically supportive." Nan recounted how he endorsed her "feeling that I probably would want to stay home for a long time or at least be home a good part of the time [because of] my desire to raise my own children," but she "was quite confident that, if I had decided to stay at work, he would have supported that as well . . . because he always enjoys hearing about going up the corporate ladder. I would come home with the same stories about these wild publishing characters and he'd get huge kicks out of it so he understood the allure and he understood the value and the fun and the challenge of the industry."

Given the concern voiced by many women for parental rather than paid care and despite their disavowal that care had to be ministered by mothers, few husbands were willing to step off the career track to allow women to continue on theirs. Regina Donofrio's husband was one of these very few: "He was very supportive. He said 'I'll do anything. I'll stay home and you work, if you don't want to leave your job.'" More commonly, husbands paid lip service to this idea, under the guise of being supportive, but like Lynn's husband who wouldn't reconfigure, they made little effort to change. Elizabeth Brand's husband was this way. When I asked her whether she and her husband, who was CEO of a beverage company associated with macho good times, had ever considered his staying home, her answer was identical to what I heard from other women and was spoken with the same undertone of indulgence and bemusement. Keeping in mind that Elizabeth was herself a high-powered consultant and a partner in her firm, her response is yet another and especially compelling illustration of the deference women accorded their husbands' careers, which they appeared not to recognize and did not acknowledge as such:

Oh yeah, he always said he would [spend more time taking care of their child]. But I don't think he would really. He
would have had to change jobs. He liked his job. And it's a
wonderful job. It's sort of a dream job for a guy.

Q: How did you get the sense that he wouldn't?

A: Well, he never did anything about it. [Laughter].

Elizabeth used humor to deflect any discomfort she might
have felt about deferring to her husband's career, or any anger
or resentment she may have had about her husband's stance
and its consequences for her career, but other women such as
Lynn were more open in their feelings. Whatever those feelings,
men's absence from the home as they were away pursuing their
careers, coupled with the preference for parental care, meant
that women were the only parent available. Women readily
stepped up to shoulder this obligation, and their sense of altru-
ism trumped—or at least soothed—any resentment they might
have felt about the asymmetry of the arrangement. This sense
of surrendering for family's sake in the face of an intransigent
spouse comes through as Leah Evans, forty-three, talks about
her decision not to pursue a "dream job offer" and instead quit
working:

So more than anything else it was just sort of what worked
for the collective whole. Even though for Leah personally, I
sort of feel like I'm the one who made the trade-off. Dick [her
husband] certainly hasn't made any trade-off at this point and
maybe eventually he will, but sort of realizing that it is a *unit*
and you've got to do it [make your decision] based on what's
best for the unit.

Women frequently overlooked the influence of prevailing
gendered norms in understanding how these were being enacted in their own families. A common strategy for justifying
why it was they, not their husbands, who needed to quit their careers to be home was to emphasize, as Elizabeth did, how much

husbands loved their jobs (as if, by inference, they did not, which for most of them was clearly not the case). Another strategy was to regard their husbands as constitutionally incapable of staying home. "He just couldn't do it," they'd say, attributing this inability to a peculiar quirk of his disposition or personality. Either way, husbands got a pass.

> *"Since Americans determine value based on occupation, the professionalization of motherhood in the new millennium serves as a strategy for at-home moms to maintain status."*

Stay-at-Home Moms Use Various Strategies to Counter Social Stigma

Karine S. Moe and Dianna J. Shandy

Mothers who make the conscious decision to stay at home to raise their children face a social stigma, according to Karine S. Moe and Dianna J. Shandy's viewpoint. Having reached this conclusion by interviewing women of various social backgrounds, the authors go on to argue that these women have found strategies of dealing with the loss of status they suffer when they leave a paying job. Some women—particularly professionals who worked several years before having children—use the language of early retirement, claiming they have "done their time" in the workforce. Other women get involved in civic affairs, volunteering for boards and various projects to improve their communities. Many mothers form networks of former working women, ensuring that they have friends

Karine S. Moe and Dianna J. Shandy, "Glass Ceilings and 100-Hour Couples: What the Opt-out Phenomenon Can Teach Us About Work and Family," pp. 114–126, University of Georgia Press, 2010. Copyright © 2010 by University of Georgia Press. All rights reserved. Reproduced by permission.

and associates who can empathize with their situation. Whichever strategies are employed, it is clear that these women do not passively accept stereotypes associated with women who "opt out" of the workforce. Moe is a professor of economics at Macalester College in Minnesota. She is the editor of Women, Family, and Work: Writings on the Economics of Gender. *Shandy is associate professor and chair of anthropology at Macalester College. In addition to Shandy's work on American families, she has researched and written on Africa, migration, and refugee resettlement.*

As you read, consider the following questions:

1. To what science fiction character do the authors compare stay-at-home moms? Why?
2. For what reasons, besides helping the community, do the women profiled in the viewpoint engage in volunteer work?
3. The viewpoint quotes a woman with three children and a Harvard MBA describing a group of ten professional women turned stay-at-home moms. From the description of this group, which profession seems to require that women keep working? Why?

When some women left their jobs, they soon discovered that they became "invisible" in social settings. A former lobbyist noted that when she tells people she's now at home with her kids, the response feels to her like, "'I could have sworn there was a person there, but I guess not.' So you really are invisible to the rest of the world. You have to have a strong ego, and you have to be willing to have people turn and walk away because you're just a mom and, so, you're boring." Another mom echoed this sentiment when she said, "It's hard on my ego to be the stay-at-home mom. . . . It's painful to see people's eyes glaze over when I say what I do." Another said, "One of the biggest challenges of being a stay-at-home parent is you have to have a really strong ego, because you essentially drop off the face of the planet as far as the rest of the world is concerned. You don't exist."

But unlike H. G. Wells's character in the science fiction novella, *The Invisible Man*, who becomes mentally unstable when he cannot become visible again, the women we interviewed resisted society's attempts to re-categorize them in some sort of diminished role when they left jobs for home. In other words, they *categorized back*. Here we look at the different ways women manage their identity in response to this societal tendency to marginalize them for their decision to stay home.

'Home, for Now' and Early Retirement

One of the key strategies women said they used to counter being relegated to the invisible focuses on the temporal aspect of their status. That is, they emphasized being home as a transitory status, or as a new phase in their life after putting in their time at work.

Some women emphasized their at-home status as a temporary hiatus from the labor force: "It's so painful. I say 'I'm home right *now*.' I think I catch myself using that modifier a lot." Another said, "I am a doctor, but taking a sabbatical for now." Whether these women intended to return to work sometime soon, sometime later, or, possibly, never, by emphasizing the provisional status of being out of the workforce they were able to better manage the reactions of people who tended to dismiss them on the basis of their employment status.

Another way women framed their experience in terms of time was to use the language of "early retirement" to describe their employment status. Not unlike senior citizens, who also struggle with similar issues of social invisibility when they exit the labor force, these women described themselves as being a "retired attorney" or "retired financial manager."

In some cases, women felt that they had achieved a high enough level of professional success to merit retirement status. One way to look at this is that when they reached a certain professional standing, they "promoted themselves" out of the workforce and into a new at-home-mom chapter of their lives. One attorney reported that practicing in her profession for over ten years gave her "the right to claim retirement status." And, it was important to these women that they had achieved this measure of success before leaving the workforce. For others, they simply felt they had been employed for pay for enough years in their life-time. And who's to say whether or not spending ten years work-ing eighty-hour weeks is equivalent to a twenty-year career work-ing forty hours per week? Kara, who had worked with the creative team in a home décor business since she graduated from college in her early twenties, simply felt like she had "put in her time" when her first baby arrived at age forty, and even more so when her second baby arrived at age forty-two, and was content to quit her job, raise her children, run the home, and provide backup for her attorney husband, who supported the family financially.

It is meaningful here to acknowledge that how these women describe their experience diverges from how others might "judge" what they are doing. A working woman in her late sixties, herself a mother and a pioneer in terms of her own educational achieve-ment, responded to our study by echoing an argument made by authors such as Linda Hirschman and Leslie Bennetts, who have written about women leaving their careers to raise children. She expressed dismay that women who had invested, and in whom so-ciety had invested, so much in terms of their educational training could take an extended break or even walk away from careers in medicine, law, or other specialized professions. What this obser-vation misses, however, is the gendered double standard at work here: men who make their money and cash out of the labor mar-ket are seen to embody the ideal of the American dream—early retirement. What signals success like a suntan in February and a 9:00 A.M. tee time? Other men who are still working would, in turn, envy him. In contrast, women who invoke early retirement are seen as suspect—most stingingly, it seems, by women who are still working.

From Housewife to Homemaker to At-Home Mom

Since Americans determine value based on occupation, the professionalization of motherhood in the new millennium serves as a strategy for at-home moms to maintain status. One can trace the evolution through the labels assigned to, and created by, women who stay home with their children. Not so long ago, women commonly used the term "housewife" to describe their exclusive role raising children and maintaining the home. That term has lost favor among women. Jan recalled, with horror, when she unthinkingly wrote "housewife" as her occupation on a form for her class of 1982 high school reunion. "It's a 1950s thing, like I'm in my high heels with an apron making meat loaf. Which, you know, that's not what I do at all. It's a horrible title because it has such a horrible stigma to it. A 'homemaker' I can handle, but 'housewife'? That's like you're the servant, just a slave. You might as well just say you're a slave." She wished that she had written "stay-at-home mom" on the form instead. "Homemaker" was also a term some of the women we interviewed used and is an accurate description that captures the breadth of responsibilities these women undertake, but most described themselves as an at-home or a stay-at-home mom. Or, in some cases, women pointedly described themselves as a stay-at-home *parent*.

Staffing the Community and Maintaining Skills

Alternatively, if they remain outside the workplace for long, women may choose to maintain a sense of occupational worth by serving in quasi-professional roles, such as on the boards of civic associations, in positions with nonprofit organizations, and as aides at their children's schools.

Some of the women frame this service in altruistic terms. One woman told us that since leaving her law practice twelve years ago, she has worked twenty-five to thirty hours per week on "some very large boards, some start-up boards, some political organizations, [and] some school-affiliated boards." She believes that she's in a privileged situation economically and this is a way to "give back to society." Another mom reported, "I have not returned to work in ten years. Frankly, I don't miss it. I also do volunteer work in the community to satisfy my need to feel that I am contributing to the world. I wouldn't change a thing!" Another woman spoke to how the various threads of self, service, and family reinforce one another in the work she does in the community and at home: "Because of family circumstances (spouse's earnings and values, choices regarding standard of living, etc.), I have had the opportunity to pursue lifelong interests and do significant work in my community while raising my children. Had I been employed full-time or part-time, I would not have had the flexibility I have needed to tend to my children's needs, nor the time to pursue my interests in community organizing and public policy."

Others view volunteer opportunities in a more utilitarian manner as a way to grow and prepare for future paid work: "Through extensive volunteer opportunities I was able to broaden and learn new abilities and skills." These skills can then be parlayed into bullet points on a future résumé. . . .

Linking back in with our discussion of strategies to maintain an identity, many use intermittent project-based work to allow them to maintain an occupational title. One at-home mother of three demonstrated this strategy: when asked how she answers the what-do-you-do question, she said "finance and homemaker," before qualifying her response with, "I did do a little bit of consulting for random firms over the years." This example illuminates how the work-status categories of full-time and part-time fail to capture the complexity of women's lived experience.

Running with a Pack of Smart Women

In recent years, surprising numbers of women with professional degrees have exited the workforce. These growing numbers

Upper-Middle-Class Women Take a Professional Approach to Raising Their Children

At certain times and places, motherhood is treated, in public discourse and by mothers themselves, very much as a profession. Motherhood is especially professionalized nowadays by a large number of American mothers, who adopt what Sharon Hays labels "the ideology of intensive mothering", which involves an eagerness to follow the advice of experts and the belief that children need to be carefully cultivated, *by their mothers*, if they are to flourish. Many contemporary mothers think of motherhood as a demanding, standards-based and knowledge-based occupation, which, though unpaid, is like professions in the kind of identification with one's work that it requires. . . . Motherhood, constructed in contemporary terms, is loaded with ideals; as a cultural ideal, it signifies far more than a biological status. One does it (at least in part) out of dedication to the enterprise and its ideals, rather than simply for material gain, which makes it more like practicing law than waiting tables or operating a forklift. The thriving industry of parenting magazines, published parenting manuals, and organizations of parents certainly treat motherhood this way. Whether or not motherhood really *is* a profession, a subset of contemporary American mothers and expert mothers'-helpers are treating it as such.

Amy B. Shuffelton, "High Stakes Motherhood and School Choice," Journal of Educational Controversy, *Summer 2010.*

are reshaping the experience of at-home motherhood. As described by one former media consultant turned at-home mom, the at-home attorney, medical doctor, veterinarian, or business executive "runs with a pack of smart women." Another at-home mom of three with a Harvard MBA [Master of Business Administration] observed: At the preschool, there are ten mothers. I know them all pretty well. Three have their law degrees but aren't practicing. One was thinking about going back, and two weren't. Four have their MBAs, and none of them are working, outside the home I should say. One had a master's in urban planning and is thinking about going back two days a week. I look around, and everybody has an advanced degree. Two of the ten are working—they are the doctors—because they have to stay current. But even they knocked [work] down to three days a week.

Therefore, it seems to be increasingly easier for younger professional women to leave work or go part-time, as other like-minded women make the same choice. The result is the formation of social networks of mothers with similar backgrounds, which provide support, occasions for adult conversation that include but are not limited to domestic issues, and opportunities for their children to play together. What characterizes these networks are the similarities in the women's education levels and the professional lives they left behind. While it may be challenging for an ex-veterinarian to grapple with the loss of professional identity when she decides to stay home with her kids, this process of adjustment is made easier when her friends and neighbors are doing it, too.

Many women, therefore, reflected on the importance of maintaining connections with other moms with similar backgrounds, as a way of negotiating the process of heading home. One told us, "I also met a group of women at an ECFE [Early Childhood Family Education] class who were all largely professional women. . . . It's this fabulous network for highly educated women to find each other in the world of 'mommydom.' . . . I think it was a really big deal to have other professional women who I spent time with when the kids were little."

The Importance of Social Networks

These social networks were an important part of the lives of at-home moms. And these women felt supported through their connections with women whom they saw as being like themselves: "It's easier to talk with people who come from a similar educational, sort of aspirational, background. A lot of that was, I think, having to do with the [subjects of the] conversations not being that stimulating themselves. It was good to have somebody to vent to who gets it—friends you can call in the middle of the night."

The importance of these social networks is not limited to the experience of women who have left high-powered careers. It was a theme in our interviews that cut across socioeconomic groupings, as seen in the words of one woman who left a mid-level management job to be home with her children: "I have a lot of really close stay-at-home mom friends that are able to do play dates and stuff. I think that especially in the summer, Seth [the interviewee's child] would be totally bored if he wasn't able to get together with friends. So that helps, that helps a lot." Relying on social networks has always been a crucial livelihood strategy for families trying to get by on a limited income or weathering uncertain economic times. In some ways the reinvigoration of social networks among women signals a return to this way of life.

"Breaking the punitive cycle of the make-or-break years will allow more mothers to stay in the game as our successful mothers did."

Planning Can Help Working Mothers Stay on the Career Fast Track

Mary Ann Mason and Eve Mason Ekman

By detouring from the traditional career path to take time out for childbirth and motherhood, professional women can damage their ability to achieve the top tier of their field. In the following viewpoint, law professor Mary Ann Mason and her daughter Eve Mason Ekman sketch several strategies for women to remain on a trajectory to reach the highest possible levels in their professions. Mason notes that other people are critical in supporting their work/family goals. In particular, they need a supportive partner at home and, at work, a mentor. Aside from maintaining these relationships, women who take time off should try to remain engaged in their field to the extent possible; working part-time at home and flexible scheduling can be key in this regard. Finally, women who leave a traditional full-time track should be prepared to gamble on any opportunity for a second chance that becomes available. In addition to teaching law, Mason is also the co-director of the Center on Economics and Family Security at the University of California, Berkeley. Mason's daughter and co-author, Eve Mason Ekman, is a social worker and photographer.

As you read, consider the following questions:

1. What percentage of highly qualified women in a study of corporate women returned successfully to full-time work after taking time off?
2. What are two essential aspects of what the author calls "mother time"?
3. What subject does the author suggest should be part of every curriculum beginning in high school and continuing through college and graduate school?

Institutional and legislative solutions are only part of the answer. As the women profiled in this book will attest, barriers to success exist not only in the workplace but also in the home. Societal stereotypes and expectations about parenting and gender play a role too. Solutions to the problem, I believe, are both personal and political.

Fortunately we now know better how mothers can plan their lives to succeed in spite of these of obstacles. The mothers in this book provide practical, personal guidelines that hold true across professions and generations. They also exhibit certainty that it can be done. They act with confidence and energy, often in the face of great resistance.

Stay in the Game

Nearly all of the successful mothers interviewed in this book took little or no time off when their children were born. They did not believe they had the option to do so and still succeed—

and they were probably right. Although 93 percent of highly qualified women want to return to work after taking time off, in a study of corporate women, only 40 percent successfully return to full-time jobs. And on average, these women lost 18 percent of their earning power when they returned to work after taking a break.

Mothers who rose to the top of their professions worked reduced schedules for a while, but as psychiatry professor Lynn Pontin related, most returned to their jobs as soon as possible, and some even brought their children to work with them in order to do so. Our research shows that mothers who have children while in graduate school and persevere without taking years out do well. In the academic world, continuing to publish, even when not fully employed, can make the difference between a permanent second tier and a second chance. Until second chances become routine institutional practice, staying close to the center of action is critical.

Breaking the punitive cycle of the make-or-break years will allow more mothers to stay in the game as our successful mothers did. The strategies described above will give the mothers a break without terminating their career plans.

Choose a Good Partner

Partners play a critical role for working mothers, but that role can be enabling or disabling. It is not a coincidence that most of the successful mothers interviewed attribute much of their accomplishment to their partners. Sometimes, as in the case of Senator Dianne Feinstein, the partner provides economic and emotional support. Other times, as in the case of Supreme Court Justice Ginsburg, the partner insists that the mother's career is equally important. Occasionally, as in the case of lawyer Carole C.'s husband, male partners break with gender stereotypes and stay at home with young children.

But many of the women we interviewed believed that partners constrained their careers. In two-career couples, women

Reentry into the Workforce Proves Difficult for Professional Women

[A Wharton Business School] study revealed that 43% of the women surveyed stayed out of the workforce longer than they expected, and 87% of those who initially never planned to return to work changed their minds, whether due to economic pressures or a reawakened desire for professional challenge. Many reentered by joining smaller companies or by shifting industries or functional roles.

[Professor Monica] McGrath and her co-authors found that the women often faced a difficult transition.

"Female executives who leave the corporate world when they hit a glass ceiling, want to raise a family full time, or decide to focus on other interests encounter frustrating roadblocks in their attempts to reenter the workforce," says McGrath, who is academic director for the Career Comeback program and also served as the former director of leadership development for the Wharton MBA program. "To overcome these obstacles, women must update their skills and stay on top of general business trends."

For those who take the off-ramp from a high-powered career, the on-ramps can be difficult to find. When they were asked to describe their hunt for a job after deciding to return to work, 50% of the survey respondents said they were frustrated and 18% said the experience was depressing. The women were "angry about having to justify the time they took off and start over as if they had never gotten an MBA," says McGrath.

Kelly J. Andrews, "On and Off Ramps,"
Wharton Magazine, *Spring 2011.*

often defer to their husband's job offer, as I did early in my career. Judith Kliman, the distinguished member of the National Academy of Sciences . . . related that following a divorce she had the freedom to advance her career by moving to a different university. And not all fathers believe that mothers should have a powerful, independent career. As one of our mothers sagely advised, "Don't marry a jerk."

An intriguing finding from our research is that single mothers do a little better than married mothers in achieving [academic] tenure. When I ask the audience what their theory is, since our data do not offer explanations, I hear such answers as "They have no choice," to "They have fewer children to take care of."

Learn Mother Time

Successful fast track mothers learn how to adapt their schedules to what I call "mother time." They must firmly negotiate reduced hours for childbirth and other family needs. And they must say no to many late meetings and some business travel. Learning to negotiate a flexible schedule without becoming marginalized is a skill some possess naturally and others can learn. Basic classes in negotiation and time management are useful if mentors are not available. "Mother time" also means making the workplace work for you. As lawyer Jessica Pers commented, "My clients don't know if I am writing a brief from my office or from home." In other words, successful mothers are skilled tacticians who know when they must put in face time at the office and when it's okay to keep a less rigid schedule.

Mind Your Mentor

As we've noted throughout this book, women on the fast track need guidance, and mentors are important at all career stages. The mothers we interviewed reported that mentors in graduate and professional schools greatly influenced their career direction. Some mentors, like my history professor, open the imagination or even the doors to the next important step. All along a career path, a mentor can make the difference between staying the course and dropping out, as did the encouragement of an older senior partner for Maryellen Herringer, the first woman in her law firm, when her clients treated her as an oddity, "like a talking dog." Mentoring is most critical during the student and make-or-break years, when women need the most help juggling career ambitions with family needs.

Mentors are not easy to find, in part because it is not usually in anyone's job description. As women rise in their careers they must make sure they bring younger women along with them and take responsibility for setting up a mentoring program in their workplace.

Mentoring about life issues should become routine in schools. Career/Life Planning 101 should be a part of every curriculum, beginning in high school and repeated in college. Forcing all young people to script out their adult lives—how they will organize their work and life and how they will achieve their ultimate goals—would assist them in planning a future in which they have real, not illusory, choices. During their graduate years, students should continue to be mentored not just for academic preparation but also for career/life preparation. Harvard University, for example, has offered a class for MBA students called Charting Your Course since 2001. It aims to help students factor in family issues to their long-range career plans. Special support is needed as students complete their training and face the job market— the danger zone period that triggers the exodus of women from the career pipeline. Women should be assisted in holding on to their professions and not veering into the second tier. Those who planned some part-time or time-out years for family would be encouraged to develop a life plan that included reentry.

Young women in science and engineering must receive special attention and encouragement from primary school onward. They should be recognized as a valuable, scarce resource in a country that is not producing enough trained technical minds to support our future growth and continued scientific innovation.

NSF [National Science Foundation] offers an Advance grant to universities that can offer innovative ways of advancing women through the competitive ranks of research science. Often a major component is an organized mentoring program. These grants have significantly changed the culture of participating universities.

Take a Chance on Second Chances

Finally, successful fast track mothers take a gamble on a second chance. In our current workplace structure, there is little encouragement for mothers who leave their careers aside for a few years to return. But most mothers don't even try. Often they lose confidence and do not apply for positions or seek out old mentors for advice and direction. But second-chance opportunities do arise, as they did for me. Maintaining contact with mentors and maintaining a foothold in the profession are the best ways to prepare for the opportunity.

Periodical and Internet Sources Bibliography

The following articles have been selected to supplement the diverse views presented in this chapter.

Kim Angie	"The Mommy Track Turns 21," *Slate*, March 31, 2010. www.slate.com.
Daniel Bates	"Emma Thompson Says You Can't Have It All," *Daily Mail Online*, (London, UK), August 3, 2010. www.dailymail.co.uk.
Melissa Johnstone and Christina Lee	"Young Australian Women's Aspirations for Work and Family," *Family Matters*, September 2009.
Arielle Kuperberg, and Pamela Stone	"The Media Depiction of Women Who Opt Out," *Gender and Society*, vol. 22, August 2008.
Meredith Melnick	"Why Women Feel More Guilt About Taking Work Home," *Time.com*, March 9, 2011. http://healthland.time.com.
Mary Pflum and Clare Shipman	"Womenomics: New Ways for Women to Aim for the Top," *ABC News*, June 3, 2009. http://abcnews.go.com.
Kelley Raina	"A Mother's Day Uprising - Why Working Moms Will Never Have Work-Life Balance," *Newsweek*, May 8, 2009.
Sarah Schutt, Wendy Crone, Paula Apfelbach, and Dawn Crim	"Lessons from the Field: Tips to Balance Life and Work," *Women in Higher Education*, vol. 30, no. 2, 2010.
Jennifer Senior	"Why Parents Hate Parenting," *New York Magazine*, July 4, 2010.
Julie C. Suk	"Are Gender Stereotypes Bad for Women? Rethinking Anti-discrimination Law and Work-Family Conflict," *Columbia Law Review*, vol. 110, January 2010.

OPPOSING
VIEWPOINTS®
SERIES

CHAPTER 2

How Do Men Balance Work and Family?

Chapter Preface

While perhaps less so than women, men do face unique difficulties in balancing the demands of work and family. Just as the legacy of their traditional role as primary caregiver to children can cause stress for working women, men face uncertainty as they struggle to adapt to new ideals of fatherhood that demand more involvement with children.

An idea of the confusion that today's fathers feel may be gleaned from results of a survey of nearly a thousand dads by researchers at the Boston College Center for Work & Family. According to the Center's June 2011 report titled "The New Dad: Caring, Committed and Conflicted," the largely white-collar respondents expressed the desire to be more involved in their children's lives as well as to take more responsibility for maintaining the household. At the same time, the fathers also wanted to be successful in their careers. The drive for a successful career is perhaps one reason why only 5 percent of new dads took more than two weeks off work after their children were born. And while nearly two-thirds of fathers maintained that men should share equal responsibility for chores such as cooking and laundry, only 30 percent reported that they themselves actually reached the ideal of spending as much time on housework as their wives.

Nevertheless, the study also showed significant changes in attitudes toward work and family balance on the part of white-collar men. The survey subjects' number one priority at work was job security, perhaps tying into results that showed fathers putting high value on providing a solid financial foundation for their family. The men were also nearly unanimous (94 percent) in stating that they would reject job offers that would interfere with their ability to spend time with their children. Further, two-thirds of the men in the study reported utilizing flextime to meet their family obligations. Nearly 50 percent of the men also reported working from home, a practice that helped them remain involved with their children. Men, however, did not usually seek to formalize either flexible schedules or working from home; they were satisfied with informal arrangements.

Overall, the study found that men were torn between a new ideal, which would have them place priority on family life and the lingering demand that men be financial providers. The study's findings also point to a way this conflict could be resolved; men who believed their companies supported their attempts to be involved fathers experienced less work-family stress. They were happier and more productive in the workplace, a result that should indicate to firms that policies encouraging involvement of fathers with their children could be beneficial for the corporate bottom line. The following viewpoints explore issues affecting men as they try to negotiate the demands of family and career.

> "This trend towards an absolute increase in child-related activities for fathers (and mothers) over recent time periods has been a repeated finding in time-budget studies."

Fathers Are Spending More Time Caring for Their Children

Margaret O'Brien

The amount of time fathers are spending with children has increased sharply since the mid-1970s, according to the viewpoint that follows. Social scientists use various methods to measure how people spend their time. One method, known as the time budget diary, asks a representative sample of the population to record their activities. Another method is to get people to estimate how they spend their time during the week—this is often used in longitudinal surveys, during which interviewees are asked the same survey questions over a span of years or even decades. The exact numbers produced by various research methods may yield different results, but according to social psychologist Margaret O'Brien, of the University of East Anglia (United Kingdom), the research all agrees that the time fathers and mothers spend interacting with children

Margaret O'Brien, "Fathers, Family Life and Work: Can Fathers Have It All?" *WELLCHI Network Conference*, Centre for Globalisation and Governance, April 1, 2006. Copyright © 2006 by Margaret O'Brien. All rights reserved. Reproduced by permission.

is increasing. In addition to her professorship, O'Brien currently co-directs the Centre for Research on the Child and Family. She researches and writes on fatherhood and work-family policy as well as initiatives to support families and children.

As you read, consider the following questions:

1. How much time per day did fathers in the mid-1970s spend with children under five, and how much did fathers in the late 1990s spend?
2. What is "weekend catch-up" as it relates to fathers and their children?
3. According to one study, how much time (on average) did American fathers interact with their under thirteen-year-old children on weekdays? On the weekend?

Amongst social science and public policy makers in Europe, there is increasing awareness of the complex and contradictory nature of contemporary fatherhood. Some commentators portray a model of 'fatherhood in transition' through the erosion of patriarchal fatherhood and an emergent caring father ideal, while others focus on the idea of 'fatherhood in crisis', a state where men are unable to either care or provide cash for their families. [Sociologist Scott] Coltrane has characterized these simultaneous trends of greater involvement and more marginality as the paradox of fatherhood. A running theme in this commentary is the 'detraditionalisation' of fatherhood whereby fathers as a social group are conceptualized as moving from a 'given' ascribed status to where fathers have more choice in constructing an 'achieved' status. Empirically there is growing evidence that fathers, particularly recent generations of fathers, are more self-conscious about juggling the different characteristics of 'the good father', particularly in terms of how they manage the conflicts between having a job and looking after the children. As [researcher] Daly has argued: This generation [of fathers] expresses a strong, family-based temporal conscience that keeps them vigilant in their fathering commitment. The value of spending time with the children has not been inherited from their own fathers but, rather, has been embraced in response to a new set of cultural conditions.

Similarly caring fathers are now part of everyday culture through advertising images and depictions of sporting icons. Fathers are expected to be accessible and nurturing as well as economically supportive to their children. . . .

Fathers' Caring Time with Children

Using time budget diary data with nationally representative data sets, most studies have shown increases in *time devoted to child care activities* for successive generations of fathers since the 1970s. Quantitative measures of fathers' involvement in childcare can be examined in absolute and relative terms. Absolute measures cover the actual time a father directly interacts with a child. In time budget diaries the amount of time spent on child-related activities as the 'main activity' is the typical measure adopted. Relative measures of father involvement estimate the proportion of time spent in childcare by fathers in comparison to mothers.

[Oxford professor Jonathan] Gershuny, using international time budget diary comparisons, has shown increased childcare time spent by British fathers since the mid-1970s, with increases especially sharp since 1985 and in particular for those men with children under age 5 years, mirroring similar trends in father childcare in the USA. Fathers of children under the age of 5 years devoted less than a quarter of an hour per day to child-related activities (as their main activity) in the mid-1970s in contrast to two hours a day by the late 1990s.

This trend towards an absolute increase in child-related activities for fathers (and mothers) over recent time periods has been a repeated finding in time budget studies and puzzles commentators concerned about time pressures in contemporary family life. A range of factors are relevant in understanding this phenomenon including: the growth in time-saving domestic technology reducing time devoted to housework, which indeed also shows a decline over time . . . and a greater awareness of children and investment in child-related activities so that children are more likely to figure in contemporary parents' diaries as 'a main activity' when accounting for their day. Reductions in leisure time, emerging as a specific time-saving strategy for contemporary parents, are a further contextual factor. For example, couples with young children, especially those working long hours, spend significantly shorter times exercising. Mothers of young children, in particular, spend less time exercising than fathers (4.25 hours in contrast to 5.05 hours per two weeks). However, despite this absolute leisure advantage to fathers, marriage and parenthood appears to also reduce men's exercise time, and much more significantly than women's (by 2.98 hours vs. 1.00 hours per two weeks lower than pre-parenthood rates), leading these authors to suggest that the norms of being a 'good husband, father, and provider' are beginning to alter modern men's time for personal leisure.

More detailed studies of time use show that the increase can also be related to 'week-end catch up' for both working mothers and fathers. These investigators found that in two-parent intact families, fathers are more engaged with their children during *weekends* than weekdays. For American children under 13 years the average time spent directly interacting with their father was 1 hour and 13 minutes on a weekday and 3.3 hours on a weekend day.

In general, for couple households there appears to be growing *gender convergence, but not equity, in parents' contribution to childcare time.* UK data are similar to the international time use diary results on levels of paternal involvement reviewed by [sociologists Joseph] Pleck and [Brian] Masciadrelli. In two-parent households with dependent children, paternal *engagement* time ranged from 1.83 to 0.62 hours per day (*between 44 per cent and 73 per cent of mothers' engagement*) and paternal *accessibility*

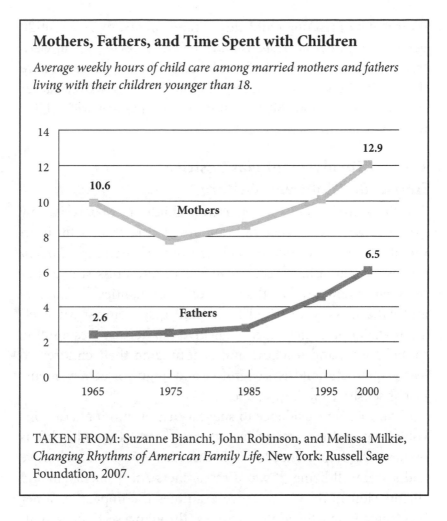

Mothers, Fathers, and Time Spent with Children

Average weekly hours of child care among married mothers and fathers living with their children younger than 18.

TAKEN FROM: Suzanne Bianchi, John Robinson, and Melissa Milkie, *Changing Rhythms of American Family Life*, New York: Russell Sage Foundation, 2007.

time ranged from 3.8 to 3.56 hours per day (*between 65 per cent to 71 per cent of mothers' accessibility*).

Assessment of paternal *responsibility* is more complex to capture. Researchers have suggested that it is a composite of 'executive function' tasks, such as arranging and planning health care appointments, which do not necessarily involve direct interaction with children, but may involve rumination and worry as well as motivation and attention. Pleck and Masciadrelli's report that levels of paternal *responsibility* in two-parent households, indicated by planning child care arrangements, to be about 20 *per cent of maternal responsibility* levels, showing an upward trend from an historic low base. It should be remembered here that researchers are describing 'responsibility in action' rather than an equal responsibility attitude, levels of which are high for both men and women. . . .

Fathers' Involvement Has Positive Impact on Children's Welfare

The literature on fathers' impact on children's welfare is now extensive and shows that children are at risk, or benefit, from the life histories both parents bring to their parenting. Current reviews of parenting practices in the round stress similarities between parents, rather than the unique qualities of mothers and fathers. As [Catherine] Lamb and [psychologist Michael] Tamis-LeMonda describe: Sensitive fathering—responding to, talking to, and teaching and encouraging their children to learn—predicts children's cognitive and linguistic achievements just as sensitive mothering does. . . .

There is some evidence to suggest that promoting father involvement and investment in the early years of a child's life is of particular importance for children's later emotional, cognitive and social well-being. [Oxford researchers Ann] Buchanan and [Erini] Flouri's British evidence examines the impact of father involvement on later adult outcomes (through a secondary analysis of 17,000 children in the National Child Development Study born in the UK in 1958 and followed up at ages 7, 11, 16, 23, 33, and age 42). The key findings from the study show that when fathers were involved with their children when the child was 7 years of age:

- it was positively related to their later educational attainment;
- children were less likely to be in trouble with the police;
- this was associated with good parent-child relationships in

adolescence and also with later satisfactory partnerships in adult life;

- it protected against an adult experience of homelessness in sons of manual workers;
- it protected children in separated families against later mental health problems.

Their analysis included resident and non-resident and biological and non-biological fathers.

Early Involvement Is Critical

The beneficial outcomes for children of earlier paternal involvement are even more striking when one considers the rather minimalist extent of involvement required for a father to be considered 'involved' with his seven-year-old child. With the narrow range of indicators of parenting available in the NCDS survey data set, Buchanan and Flouri defined an 'involved' father as one who: read to his child 'most weeks' (37% of fathers); were rated by teachers as being 'very interested' in their child's education (44% of fathers); took their child on outings 'most weeks' (73% of fathers) and took an equal role to mother in the management of their children (60 % of fathers).

Moreover, involvement levels at seven appeared to be continuous over the life course, in that early father involvement with a child was associated with continuing involvement (using age appropriate indicators) with that child throughout childhood and adolescence. . . .

Studies assessing the impact of father involvement in the early years on later child outcomes confirm the importance of *early paternal investment* in caring.

> "Even if employers are open to dads
> spending more time with junior, there
> are tradeoffs for fathers. For example, it
> may be harder to get the top jobs."

Men Are Discouraged from Work Flexibility and Parental Leave

Eve Tahmincioglu

The following viewpoint outlines some of the difficulties men face in trying to take time out from their careers to care for children. Men are less likely than women to formally request flexible work hours, relying instead on improvised arrangements. Perhaps more significantly, they are reluctant to take advantage of their rights under the Family and Medical Leave Act (FMLA), which requires employers to offer new parents up to twelve months unpaid leave upon the birth of a child. In corporate America, according to the author, there is still an assumption that women will take parental leave; men sense that their careers will be hurt if they exercise their legal rights under FMLA. Eve Tahmincioglu writes the "Your Career" column for MSNBC.com and has been a regular contributor to the New York Times. *She is the author of the book,* From the Sandbox to the Corner Office: Lessons Learned on the Journey to the Top.

As you read, consider the following questions:

1. How does the Chupick family deal with the smaller paycheck that comes from the fathers working flexible hours?
2. According to consulting firm Work+Life CEO Cali Yost, what proportion of men are looking for flexible hours in order to balance home life and work?
3. What percentage of men and women, respectively, take a "scenic route" (taking some time off or reducing their hours) at some stage in their career?

More dads are starting to stand up and ask for more flexible work arrangements—from time off after a baby is born to reduced hours and days. Such options were once thought to be a mother's domain, but now an increasing number of dads want to be more hands-on in raising their kids. Others are driven by economics: a wife might earn more money or not have flexibility at work.

"It's changing pretty quickly, thanks to the changing dynamics of the work force," said Jamie Ladge, assistant professor of management and organizational development at Northeastern University and co-author of a new study on working dads released last week called "The New Dad: Exploring Fatherhood within a Career Context." "Women are more than half of the workforce, and most of the layoffs we've seen in this downturn have been in mostly male-dominated jobs. So men are having to step up."

The result? "You're seeing many more dads at school at drop off and pick up," Ladge said.

In Search of Flexibility

Of course, working fewer hours also means a smaller paycheck. On top of that, the recession has added to stress over family finances and increased expectations to perform at work.

"My rule of thumb in our household is we try to have two incomes but we live as if there's one," said [media director Jason]

Chupick. "We also have a tiny mortgage and have cut back as much as we could."

Despite having flexible hours, Chupick works harder than he ever did before, writing a blog, updating his skills, and going to industry events. "You have to stay employable."

Like working mothers, a large number of working fathers are also looking for the elusive work-life balance.

"Men are just as likely as women to want flexibility," said Cali Yost, CEO of consulting firm Work+Life Fit Inc. Her nationally representative annual Work+Life Fit Reality Check survey found that 90 percent of men were looking for flexible hours to help balance work and home life, compared to 92 percent among women.

And some men are leaving work behind altogether when kids come along, said Sylvia Ann Hewlett, economist and founder of the Center for Work-Life Policy, a process she calls off-ramping.

"Over the last five years, there's been a doubling of the percentage of men who off-ramp for reasons of child care—and nearly double for those who off-ramped for eldercare reasons," she said.

And, she added, 38 percent of men, compared to 58 percent of women, take a "scenic route, stepping back without stepping out."

"Increasingly men are 'ramping down'—working from home Friday afternoons or staggering their hours in order to pick up more domestic responsibilities," she said. "This is particularly true in households where wives out-earn their husbands. These households are on the rise as the Great Recession clobbered men more than women."

Corporate America Still Catching Up

Steve Moore, a human resource specialist at Administaff, believes the desire for more work-life balance is a generational thing but not a gender thing.

For those under 30, he said, "it seems that some traditional stereotypes are starting to lessen just a bit in terms of who's responsible for care of the children."

But Yost maintained that corporate America has not caught up with this reality.

"Time and again, companies primarily address how to manage work-life issues and use flexibility in the 'women's initiative' even though the policies and programs that are in place are theoretically intended for everyone," she said.

That may explain why men are more likely to seek informal flexibility in the workplace.

According to "The New Dad" study:

> The fathers were far more likely to exercise informal flexibility rather than ask for a formal flexible work arrangement. While many of the men did use flexibility to be available to share childcare responsibilities, or attend physician's appointments, this was always done in an informal or 'stealth' fashion. Virtually none of the men felt a lack of support from their manager or co-workers when utilizing flexibility.

Indeed, there is still a stigma for working dads who are looking for the flexibility many moms have been requesting for years.

"Certainly you get snide remarks from men occasionally," said Marc Vachon, who does IT support for a market research company called Chadwick Martin Bailey. He works a reduced workweek, with Wednesdays off so he can spend time with his preschool son.

Vachon, who's been touting the benefits of shared parenting for years and recently wrote a book on the topic, "Equally Shared Parenting: Rewriting the Rules for a New Generation of Parents," said men need to step up and ask for flexibility no matter what society thinks. "From my perspective, the hurdles are mostly personal as opposed to systemic and institutional."

Equal Rights to Parental Leave

When it comes to the law, men are supposed to be treated equally with women when they ask for reduced hours or time off.

For example, under the Family and Medical Leave Act [FMLA], men are also eligible to take an unpaid leave of absence after a baby is born or after an adoption, said Ashley Brightwell, a labor lawyer with Alston & Bird, who said she's seeing more men taking advantage of protections under FLMA.

"Employers need to treat employees taking leave the same," she said. "Decisions need to be made regardless of gender."

Unfortunately, she said, that's not always the case. "There is certainly prejudice out there. A lot of employers assume, especially in the context of a birth, that the mother is going to need time off. They are not typically as understanding when tables are turned and dad wants to take time off."

Even if employers are open to dads spending more time with junior, there are tradeoffs for fathers. For example, it may be harder to get the top jobs.

"Work is important to me, but the corner office is not my goal," said Vachon. "My goal is to have a sustainable, enjoyable life."

Just as moms have known for years, maintaining work-life balance is extremely difficult.

"Certainly, there are a lot of challenges with younger children, a lot of stress and chaos," said [Michael] Sherman, the attorney from Mobile who scaled back his work life to spend more time with his kids.

He plans to ramp up his work again in the fall, but stick to 30 hours a week so he can arrange his home-schooling schedule accordingly.

Sherman's wife, Kathy, is a full-time, in-house corporate attorney. Sherman said he has gotten some odd looks from people who find out about their reversed roles, especially from men who can't see themselves in such a role even though they may be longing for more time with family.

"If the reason they're not doing it is out of some sense of pride or ego, they may be sorry in the long run that they missed an opportunity to strengthen that connection with their kids," he said.

> "Throughout all 33 interviews, not a single concern was expressed in the workplace that fatherhood would somehow interfere with or diminish a new father's career focus."

Managerial Support Helps Fathers Balance Work and Family

Brad Harrington, Jamie Ladge, and Fred Van Deusen

Based on interviews with white-collar working fathers, the following viewpoint presents evidence that these men are generally happy with the work-life support their companies or organizations offer. While the men may be expected at times to work long hours, they are also able to be flexible with their schedules when needed. In contrast to the formal family support arrangements many women reach with employers, the men's approaches regarding time off for family are generally informal. Fatherhood also had unexpected career benefits, with the men reporting that having a child enhanced how they were perceived at work. Brad Harrington is the executive director of the Center for Work and Family (CWF) at Boston

Brad Harrington, Jamie Ladge, and Fred Van Deusen, "The New Dad: Exploring Fatherhood Within a Career Context," pp. 21–24, Center for Work and Family, Boston College, 2010. Copyright © 2010 by Boston College. All rights reserved. Reproduced by permission.

College and an associate research professor in the college's Carroll School of Management. Jamie Ladge is an assistant professor of management and organizational development at Northeastern University. Her research focuses on identity, careers, and family within organizations. Fred Van Deusen is a senior research associate at the Center for Work and Family. He was formerly an executive with Hewlett-Packard.

As you read, consider the following questions:

1. When the men interviewed for the study did have problems combining work and family, what was the primary difficulty concerning?
2. In research on working parents, who in the company hierarchy is held to be most important for an employee's ability to balance work and family?
3. According to the viewpoint, why might younger managers be more understanding of work-family challenges?

With all of the changes taking place in the fathers [participating in the study] as individuals, and in their relationships at home, we wanted to also explore how these changes were impacting fathers in the workplace. For the most part, the fathers in our study found their workplace experiences quite positive. Many fathers had adjusted their schedules and the total number of hours they worked to make more time for their family responsibilities. In general, their bosses and work cultures supported the informal flexibility that they needed. Some found it difficult to combine work and family, primarily because of the number of hours they had to work, often in connection with a demanding job, boss, or office culture.

Workplace Responses

We asked participants to reflect on the overall experiences of becoming a father in an organizational context. We found that virtually all of the men in our study had very positive experiences. As one participant put it, "*My organization is not inhibiting me from being the kind of father I want to be.*"

One of the questions we explored was, "*Did becoming a father change how others perceived or responded to you?*" Most felt that becoming a father had a positive impact on how others saw them in the workplace. About half said the difference was minor and half felt it was more significant. Even in the cases where the changes were deemed minor, they were nonetheless positive:

> "I think it does have a little impact. You put a picture on your desk and it encourages people who probably would never have stopped by to say, oh, tell me about your son. So it's a social thing, it's only a positive." [Evan]

Becoming a father seemed to have "softened the edges" and made it easier for individuals to be seen as approachable and accessible. The men often felt they were able to make better social connections with others at work who are parents. They felt they were now "members of the parenting club." As Patrick, a manager in an insurance firm stated, "*I'm developing relationships with people at work that you probably wouldn't have if you didn't have a child. It's such a big thing and establishes a common rapport.*"

Another very important dimension of becoming a father was the view that being a father granted an individual a greater aura of credibility, maturity and responsibility. This theme was echoed by many participants. They felt they were viewed as more serious (in a career sense) by their peers. Mark, a consultant, stated that "*I think it makes people think, it gives them the perception I'm older or more mature than before.*" Patrick also commented "*It definitely feels like people would be more apt to give me more responsibility.*" This was echoed by Sam who also made reference to a common perception that you are now considered as a member of the club, "*I thought it would be positive. They would look at me as '[Sam's] finally getting serious. He's now one of us, one of the club members.'*"

The overarching message from the interviewees was that there was a difference in how they were perceived, and this difference was virtually always positive. Throughout all 33 interviews, not a single concern was expressed in the workplace that fatherhood would somehow interfere with or diminish a new father's career focus. This stands in stark contrast to the reaction which many women perceive upon becoming a new mother. Recent research reinforced the view that when women become mothers, they are often perceived as not only less committed to their careers, but also surprisingly less competent and less promotable. By contrast, the men in our study reported no negative ramifications of their change in status to father and in fact strongly suggested that reactions were exclusively positive in terms of how they were perceived by their employer.

Manager Support of Work-Family Balance

A major concern (almost pre-occupation) in the work-life literature and research regards the degree of support that people feel they receive from their direct manager. Even in organizations that enjoy outstanding reputations as "family friendly", many individuals are reluctant to raise their work-family concerns or desires with their manager out of fear that they will be seen as less committed to their work and their employer. This concern is so widespread that it has been studied and termed the "implementation gap" between espoused work-life policies and actual practice.

Given this concern, we were pleasantly surprised that the majority of the fathers in our study spoke in very positive terms of how supportive their manager was on work-family issues. Only a handful said that they did not feel supported. While virtually all of the fathers in our study were using informal flexibility (i.e. they had not requested or been granted a formal change in their schedules), they felt their managers were quite supportive of the work-life challenges they faced. As Evan, an analyst in the financial services industry stated:

"My boss is extremely understanding, has had no problems with me taking time to do all the stuff I needed to do. We have both men and women in my area who work 3-day work weeks or work from home on Mondays and come in the rest of the week."

This support seemed to extend to not only the challenges faced by new fathers, but also other work–family issues as well. Grant, an area sales manager for a large information provider, reflected on his own circumstances, but also those of a close colleague who was in the middle of a divorce:

"A colleague of mine is going through a divorce right now. And . . . talk about [a boss] being supportive. It's always nice to be supportive in good times when you have kids. [But] she's super supportive of this guy, and he is really on the ropes right now."

It may be that what we are seeing reflects the trends in the larger society where younger managers, who are much more likely than the previous generation to be in two-career couples or single parent families, have a higher level of understanding for the work-family challenges that such employees face. In addition, the challenging economic environment of the past year, coupled with the extremely high level of downsizing that has occurred, may be giving managers greater empathy as well. As Patrick stated in describing his own manager's situation:

"He's got three kids of his own, a great family and he understands the balance necessary. I think he's actually had an epiphany in the past couple of years. He's been handling a lot with the company shrinking . . . feeling a little overwhelmed. He bought a house on the Cape that he sort of uses as a refuge. I think he and his family have re-discovered themselves basically."

Ease of Combining Work and Family

When asked, more than half of our participants stated that their current roles made it relatively easy to combine work and family.

"So far it's proven to be fairly easy. I'm pretty fortunate in that the people that I work with also have families. So, there's a lot of general understanding in the office as to what it actually takes to have a family, which is nice." [Anthony]

"I have a laptop and I'm not tied to a specific location to do work. There aren't a lot of occasions where I have to work late into the night or on weekends." [Peter]

Various forms of flexibility, mostly informal, greatly facilitated this. Flexibility was mentioned by most of the participants as being important to successfully combine work and family, in addition to a supportive boss and a supportive culture.

"I think the organization is very overt in its espoused values around work life balance. I think that the leadership in my area supports a strong work life balance, and is willing and flexible. My manager's very willing and flexible—willing to make accommodations and allow me to do whatever I need to do to meet the needs of my family when necessary." [Tom]

"I would say it has been easy. And it's less the job, because I know other people who have my job who feel like they can't, or have decided that they can't do it and have a family. In my particular case, my employer has been very accommodating in allowing me flexibility when I'm here, and then also is understanding on days when my kid is sick or something comes up, where they understand that as long as I get the work done, they're fine if I'm not in the office as much. So my employer has been outstanding on that." [Tim]

For those that did not find it easy to combine work and family, the primary issue they raised was the number of hours they had to work, often in connection with a demanding job, boss, or office culture.

> *"Men tell stories of being excluded from mothers' groups and hearing of police questioning fathers seen hanging around the playground."*

Finances Factor into Increase in Stay-at-Home Dads

Katherine Shaver

In the viewpoint that follows, journalist Katherine Shaver looks at the growing phenomenon of stay-at-home dads—married men who stay at home with their children while their wives work. While most of the husbands interviewed by Shaver enjoy the time with their children, the main reason they have opted to stay home is financial—their spouses have bigger paychecks or more promising careers. The men do find themselves in an ambiguous situation, praised for their decision to remain at home but sometimes excluded from mother-dominated playgroups or viewed with suspicion by their working-male peers. Shaver is a Washington Post *reporter who focuses on the DC Metro area.*

As you read, consider the following questions:

1. What percentage of stay-at-home parents are fathers,

and how much did this percentage increase in the decade prior to this viewpoint's publication date?

2. According to federal labor statistics, what proportion of men act as their children's primary caregiver?

3. When—in terms of their children's lives—do many of the stay-at-home dads intend to return to work?

It could have been any play group in the Washington area, except for the diaper bags. No Vera Bradley flowers, no pastel polka dots. The bags lying around Matt Vossler's Rockville living room Tuesday afternoon were dark Eddie Bauer canvas. One was red but, as its owner quickly pointed out, "very metrosexual."

"Potty training was a lot of angst for me," Vossler, 43, a one-time paralegal, told the group.

"Bottle feeding was my angst," said Matt Trebon, 36, a former Capitol Hill staffer, as his 3-year-old daughter nuzzled his side.

"And trying to get them to eat well," Vossler continued, bringing up his 6-year-old. "Martin is all carbs."

"Eight days—no diapers!" Trebon suddenly announced, thrusting his fists into the air.

With their wives as breadwinners, the fathers are part of a small but growing group of men who are quitting or retooling their careers to stay home with their children.

Rapid Growth in Stay-at-Home Dads

On Father's Day, an estimated 159,000 stay-at-home dads, or 2.7 percent of the country's stay-at-home parents—almost triple the percentage from a decade ago—will celebrate what has become a full-time job, according to the U.S. Census Bureau. But experts say that number should be far higher because the census definition doesn't consider single fathers, those with children over 15 or those who work part-time or flexible hours to be home. Federal labor statistics show the number of fathers providing their young children's primary care is more like one in five.

New Family Roles Mean More Stress for Men

In 2002, the Families and Work Institute reported that while women felt about the same level of frustration when it came to balancing work and life over the last 25 years, men's frustration sharply rose—from 34 percent of men in dual-earning couples reporting a conflict in 1977 to 54 percent in 2002.

"It's probably because their [men's] roles are newer," said Ellen Galinsky, president and co-founder of the Families and Work Institute. "They're less likely to have role models. When women first started working, they felt like they were pioneers and now I think you're seeing that feeling among men."

Jen Brown, "'Daddy Wars': Fathers Strike Back," ABCNews.com, March 8, 2006. http://abcnews.go.com.

Those fathers are changing the way many children are growing up and the calculations families make as they try to balance busy and often conflicting lives. "Men have started to join the struggle of how you juggle family and work," said sociology professor Andrea Doucet, who studies Canadian stay-at-home fathers at Carleton University in Ottawa.

Stay-at-home dads now have Web sites, blogs such as "A Man Among Mommies," support groups and an annual convention. They are showing up in "Mommy and Me" classes and PTA meetings. Many men's restrooms now have diaper-changing tables, and companies market souped-up strollers with brand names such as "the Bob."

Those in the Washington region who have lived elsewhere say they sense more of their kind here because of the prevalence of high-powered working women. DCMetroDads, a group started nine years ago, has 325 members.

Publishers and TV talk shows have made a cottage industry out of the "Mommy Wars" debate and the angst of motherhood. But stay-at-home dads are subject to relatively little study and, unlike their wives, generally don't care that their 6-year-old is still wearing pajama bottoms at 3 P.M.

Sometimes, society goes easy on them.

Praise and Criticism

"Dads get so much credit for staying home with the kids," said Eric Hazell, 43, of Bowie, who returned to a professorship at the University of Maryland in 2004 after two years with his children. "If moms work, they have possible guilt for not being home with their kids. If they're home, there's a lot of tug that they're sacrificing their career. For dads, people think it's just great that you stay home. Then when we go back [to work], it's what people expect in the first place."

Other times, staying home can be tricky.

Men tell stories of being excluded from mothers' groups and hearing of police questioning fathers seen hanging around the playground. Some have found close friends among stay-at-home mothers, while others say they don't feel comfortable with such socialization or fear their wives would disapprove.

Some fathers, particularly black men, say they have gone years without meeting another stay-at-home dad.

"There could be hundreds of kids [at a playground], and I'm sitting on the bench with my Blackberry," said Phil Rawlings, 42, of Upper Marlboro, who quit an 18-year paralegal career last fall to stay home with his 4-year-old. "I look around to keep an eye on Tyler, and there's nothing but moms."

Many of his friends don't understand his decision, he said, even though he works from home 35 to 40 hours per week as a consultant.

"I quit a perfectly good six-figure job," Rawlings said. "My friends asked me if I got fired. It's unreal among black men. You don't stay home from a good job to be with your kids."

Most stay-at-home fathers say the decision boiled down to money: Their wives had fatter paychecks or more promising careers. Many say relying on one income has meant a more modest home, older cars and fewer vacations. Few opt out completely; many say they work part-time from home.

A Financial Decision

Jeff Miller and his wife, Shawn Brennan, both worked from their Silver Spring home after their first child was born. When they needed more money, Brennan took a full-time Montgomery County government job. Miller, 40, could continue as a lower-paid, part-time business professor at the University of Maryland, while his flexible home consulting business let him care for Bennett, now 7, and Megan, 5. Miller said he knows four other stay-at-home dads in his neighborhood.

"Today when I get back, I'll make a pot roast," he said Wednesday morning as he boiled pasta for Megan's picnic lunch with some preschool friends. After mixing Megan's "mystery cereal"—his own concoction of three cereals and nuts for extra protein—Miller pulled her hair into a ponytail, pointed her toward a flowered sundress to put on and loaded her into his Chrysler convertible.

At the park, one of the picnic mothers had brought sanitary wipes and a Dora the Explorer blanket, on which little girls ate sandwiches, corn on the cob and cut-up fruit. Megan sat on the grass eating her buttered pasta from a thermos. "I didn't really bring a bowl for you," Miller said apologetically. She didn't seem to care.

Miller said he has never defined himself by his job. Still, when someone asks what he does, he often finds himself first mentioning his teaching and consulting.

"It's not like I can't do laundry or make a pot roast," he said. "That's the easy stuff. It's more like do I want a job or deal with the societal stuff of people saying 'Dude, what do you do again? You stay home with your kids?'"

His wife said knowing he's there gives her peace of mind, even if her children sometimes end up calling her "Daddy" after a long day. "I like them having a good relationship with him," Brennan said.

Still, she said, when her father came home from work, he relaxed with the newspaper while her mother prepared dinner. She said she sometimes doesn't have time to change out of her office clothes before she's cooking and washing dishes that piled up in her absence. ("I'm terrible," Miller confessed of his housework.)

"There are times when I think if I sat here and added up all the hours I'm with the kids, I think I'm pretty much with them as much as he is," Brennan said. "When I'm home, I kind of take over."

Like their female counterparts, most stay-at-home fathers say they plan to return to work, many when their youngest child reaches kindergarten. But many said they will look for limited hours and flexible schedules.

They say they don't want to lose the intimacy, the way they have come to know their children's daily rhythms like no one else. Several pointed out that they are the first to wake up when their children cry out in the night. Some call it their mother's intuition.

> "Mothers may also serve a 'gatekeeping' role in the family, effectively limiting the involvement of fathers in activities [that] have traditionally been seen as belonging to mothers."

Mothers Are Key to Promoting Father Involvement

Kerry Daly, Lynda Ashbourne, and Linda Hawkins

The authors of this viewpoint describe how fathers' roles in the family are both diverse and changing rapidly. This can create stresses within the family, as parenting and other household tasks are increasingly—either voluntarily or out of necessity—done by fathers. Women often hold a position of power as couples renegotiate their duties in what the authors call the "micropolitics" of care. The three authors of this viewpoint are all associated with the University of Guelph (Canada). Kerry Daly is a professor in the Department of Family Relations and Applied Nutrition. Aside from his interest in work and family issues, he is also an expert in qualitative research in the social sciences. Lynda Ashbourne is a professor in the Family Relations and Human Development program and focuses on teen-parent relationships. Linda Hawkins is the executive director

Kerry Daly, Lynda Ashbourne, and Linda Hawkins, "Work-Life Issues for Fathers," *Handbook of Work-Family Integration*, pp. 249–266, Elsevier, 2008. Copyright © 2008 by Elsevier Science Publishers BV. All rights reserved. Reproduced by permission.

of the university's Centre for Families, Work and Wellbeing. She has contributed to the Ivey Business Journal.

As you read, consider the following questions:
1. What, according to the authors, suggests that men tend to look at work-family balance as a private issue?
2. What are some of the fundamental questions that, according to the authors, must be asked in order to understand why men often remain marginal when it comes to caring for the family?
3. What is the objective of the authors' work-family agenda for men?

There is considerable evidence to indicate that in dual earner homes, mothers are more likely than fathers to be involved in carrying out activities associated with the "responsibility dimension" of parental care. As a result, the responsiveness of fathers to the needs of their children is frequently negotiated with mothers. When fathers are resident in the family home, household tasks and parenting are negotiated, often in the context of dual-earning couples, along with work-related tasks. Mothers are more likely to negotiate flexibility with respect to work requirements and to be more aware of employee family-related benefits. This gender difference may effectively allow fathers to take a less active and engaged role in taking responsibility for childcare and in the area of negotiating and making the work/family interface more manageable for the couple and family. . . .

The Role of Women in Facilitating Father Involvement

Mothers may also serve a "gatekeeping" role in the family, effectively limiting the involvement of fathers in activities [that] have traditionally been seen as belonging to mothers. In family structures where parents have new and former partners, there can be varying degrees of involvement of biological parents and step-parents/new partners. Frequently such involvement is governed by issues of residence and proximity, as well as divorce agreements, and stepmothers may continue to take on gendered and traditional caring roles of women, acting to either facilitate or block the involvement of fathers. It may be that men view such action or attitudes as either facilitating their negotiation of work and family, or as presenting obstacles to their involvement in the family. . . .

In order to move forward with a conceptualization of work and family issues that is also rooted in men's experience, we feel that it is necessary to consider a number of key issues.

Work-Life Integration for Men

First, it is evident that while men experience high levels of work-life conflict, they are less likely than women to pursue flexibility strategies as a way of reducing this conflict. This would suggest that work-life conflict for men is more likely to be experienced as a personal trouble rather than a public issue. In other words, men feel the conflict and contend with the competing pressures but, in general, operate in environments that rarely recognize the presence of the conflict or the need for resolution. Environments include work cultures where men are not expected to need flexibility to respond to family needs—and the broader cultures of masculinity and fatherhood that continue to hold mothers at the center of the parenting experience. In the absence of cultural supports for fathers to be at the center of their children's lives, work-life balance issues for men are confined to the realm of private troubles that require personal and private solution. If there is a desire for men to become more fully engaged providers of care in families, it is first necessary to make the challenge of men's work-life balance into a public issue. This is a change that must occur on many levels including: individual men turning their private troubles into a public issue (by speaking out about their needs and asserting their entitlement to parental leaves or

Fathers' Roles in Childcare Are Often Invisible

Cultural dominance of the mother's role in the provision of care to children leaves fathers' emerging role as carer somewhat invisible. A sole focus on women's experience blinds us to the type and depth of the emerging participation of men, rendering men's care not only less visible, but also less valuable. Many fathers now do hands-on care work formerly assigned to women in the family, including diaper changing, daycare drop off, and medical and school appointments. Father participation and interest in involvement may indeed be changing faster than our ability to measure and report these changes—certainly father involvement is changing faster than our dated discourse on father providers and mother nurturers.

Kerry Daly and Linda Hawkins, "Fathers and the Work-Family Politic," Ivey Business Journal, *July-August 2005.*

flexibility strategies); work organizations opening conversations about men's levels of work-life conflict and their needs for support; and communities playing a greater role in recognizing the value and importance of father involvement (for children, partners, families, and community well-being).

Second, work-life challenges for fathers are as diverse as the circumstances within which men carry out their fathering responsibilities. In thinking broadly about work-life strategies for men it is important to recognize the many types of fathering and the needs that might arise from those diverse experiences (e.g., immigrant fathers, fathers of children with special needs, single fathers). The kinds of strategies that would effectively support fathers in being more fully involved with their children are contingent on whether they can be truly flexible in meeting circumstances, including challenges of the age of children and daily schedules of childcare and school, the level and timing of access that the father has when working and parenting under custody arrangements, or the nature of the co-parenting relationship that is shaped by its own rhythms and schedules.

Third, it is important to look at men's experience of work-life within a systemic, contextualized perspective. Given the rootedness of work-life issues in women's experience, there is a temptation to simply extend this thinking to men's experience—to borrow the template from women, build on the best practices and ensure that men are provided with similar opportunities to balance their work and family lives. However, in an effort to balance work and family lives, the issue is not always what individual mothers or fathers need—rather the issue is how to arrange patterns of work and family care so that family systems can function in optimal ways. When it comes down to the everyday challenge of "fitting it all in", gender differences may be over-shadowed by a picture of women and men who were working collaboratively to manage the challenges on the home and the work front. Fathering and mothering are seen then not as separate activities, as the experience of parenting is "created in the shared goings-on between people in the course of their lives through intervals of negotiating, competing, compromising and rearranging". Even in families where parents are living apart, there are a variety of challenges that require collaborative efforts in order to accommodate changing schedules and respond to emerging needs.

Women and Family 'Micropolitics'

Thinking systemically also means taking into account the centrality of women's role in orchestrating family life. In contrast with an individual level question that seeks to find out "why men resist change?", a systemic question would endeavour to look at the ways in which both women and men hold to traditional patterns of parenting that keep women at the center and men on the margins. Efforts to understand why men do or don't engage in work-life initiatives must take into account the underlying motives, beliefs, and values that are part of the participating family system. This involves fundamental questions about whether men can be trusted to undertake the role of primary parent (e.g., with a newborn), whether men are perceived as capable and competent as mothers in carrying out the parenting role, and whether mothers themselves are willing to release some of their own responsibilities that are rooted in the high standards of mothering ideology.

The final issue is to think about work-family issues for men as embedded in a micropolitics of care. If part of the feminist objective was to bring public recognition to the importance of paid labor for women's social status and influence, then a parallel objective in a work-family agenda for men is to bring recognition to the importance of care activity for the well-being of children, partners, and men themselves. Whereas women in our discussions seem predisposed to provide care, men must somehow learn how to provide care. By way of illustration, we are more likely to be preoccupied with how men learn to be a father whereas for women it is taken for granted or assumed that they know how to be a mother. A micropolitics of care, as part of the work-life agenda for men, is more concerned with the ways that women and men navigate the gendered territories of mothering and fathering and work towards fairness and equity in both their relationship and their care responsibilities. It involves the degree to which co-parents choose models that are either interchangeable (based on assumptions that both parents should be able to move seamlessly into a full spectrum of parenting tasks) or complementary (where they decide to build on individual strengths when providing care). It involves negotiation about time and the responsibility for making decisions about family time. Partners in shared parenting bring preferences about pace, rhythm, and activity to interaction and through a process of negotiation, they adjust and coordinate their activity patterns with one another. This is consistent with a relational perspective where taking responsibility for children and domestic life cannot be reduced to time allocations only, but rather involves attention to the navigation of complex, gendered caring responsibilities in relationships. This includes not only providing care to children, but also looking at the way that fathers extend that care to their parenting partners in order to keep relationships strong.

Periodical and Internet Sources Bibliography

The following articles have been selected to supplement the diverse views presented in this chapter.

Greg Beato	"Real Men Cry and Do Laundry," *Slate*, October 11, 2010. www.slate.com.
Brian Braiker	"Just Don't Call Me Mr. Mom—This Generation of Fathers Is More Involved in Child Care Than Ever," *Newsweek*, October 8, 2007.
Jen Brown	"'Daddy Wars': Fathers Strike Back," *ABC News*, March 8, 2006. http://abcnews.go.com.
Andrew Romano and Tony Dokoupil	"Men's Lib—to Survive in a Hostile World, Guys Need to Embrace Girly Jobs and Dirty Diapers. Why It's Time to Reimagine Masculinity," *Newsweek*, September 27, 2010.
Michael Douglas	"The Role of a Lifetime," *Newsweek*, September 15, 2007.
Nancy Gibbs	"Viewpoint: Bring on the Daddy Wars," *Time*, February 27, 2006.
Katherine Lewis	"Why Do Dads Lie on Surveys About Fatherhood?" *Slate*, June 17, 2010. www.slate.com.
Raising Children Network	"Work and Family: Dads Finding a Balance," 2010. raisingchildren.net.au.
Joel Schwartzberg	"Slouching toward Fatherhood," *Newsweek*, April 13, 2009.
Mike Tomlin	"Fatherhood Comes First, Then the Game," *USA Today*, 2009. www.usatoday.com.
Jack Welch	"On Work and Family," *Newsweek*, April 4, 2005.

OPPOSING
VIEWPOINTS®
SERIES

CHAPTER 3

How Do Government Policies Affect the Work-Family Balance?

Chapter Preface

Men and women's efforts to balance work and family life are influenced by society. Societal attitudes affect individuals' choices regarding child bearing and child care arrangements. The views of friends, family, and peer groups certainly influence whether a mom or dad will stay home with the children or pursue full or part-time employment. In addition government policy can have a major impact on familial decisions. Many industrialized countries have decided to ease the burdens on new mothers and fathers by mandating paid maternity leave, often in an effort to boost birthrates. But the costs associated with such policies, economic difficulties, and cultural factors have prevented these policies from being adopted in America, which requires only unpaid maternity leave, and even this mandate applies only to companies with fifty employees or more.

The economic difficulties of the late 2000s and early 2010s have certainly put pressure on American businesses to cut costs, with paid maternity leave being a prime candidate for elimination. A survey by the Society for Human Resource Management found that 17 percent of the businesses surveyed offered paid maternity leave, but that 7 percent of businesses planned to reduce or eliminate the benefit. That is, 40 percent of the already small number of businesses that paid for mothers to take time off at the birth of children were planning to decrease or entirely cut these benefits. In an August 2010 *Boston Globe* article, Megan Woolhouse and Katie Johnston Chase wrote about the difficulties local businesses were having in offering parental leave benefits. The reporters quoted the owner of a maternity store who said she would like to offer three months of paid leave but "that's just not an economic reality right now . . . some months, my husband and I don't get paychecks."

The situation is quite different in other industrialized nations. New Swedish parents, for example, are eligible for sixteen months of leave, paid at 80 percent of their working wages. In British Columbia, Canada, fourteen months of paid leave are available for new mothers. In the United States, businesses that fear the cost of paid family leave have prevented the adoption of such policies. As Michael Eastman, the director of labor policy for the United States Chamber of Commerce, put it in a July 2006 Associated Press article, "There are a couple of central problems when we look at paid leave legislation. The first is: who's paying for it?"

Cultural factors also play a part in American policy makers' continued rejection of paid parental leave. In Europe maternity leave was seen as a woman-friendly policy, something which feminists should support, whereas in the United States feminists "didn't want to hear anything about mothers," according to Columbia professor Jane Waldfogel. "They wanted equal rights for women and didn't emphasize special treatment." In Europe maternity leave is also seen as helping to maintain the population, while in America immigration ensures continued population growth.

The bottom line is that the United States remains one of the only advanced industrial economies that does not offer parents paid time off from their jobs to care for newborn children. However, there are those in the United States who continue to push for "family-friendly" government policies, some of which are debated in the following viewpoints.

> "Even when workers have the right and
> the means to take time off, corporate
> culture pressures them not to."

Government Support for Work-Family Balance Is a Myth

Ellen Bravo

In the viewpoint that follows, Ellen Bravo presents evidence that federal legislation intended to help working mothers and fathers has been ineffective. The 1978 Pregnancy Discrimination Act forbid employers from firing women who got pregnant, but did not prevent businesses from filling a woman's job permanently while she was on maternity leave. One of the goals of 1993's Family and Medical Leave Act (FMLA) was to correct this situation by guaranteeing workers six weeks of maternity or paternity leave. However the FMLA did not apply to businesses with less than fifty employees—40 percent of private sector workers were left uncovered. Further, the law required that companies provide only unpaid leave; hourly workers often cannot afford the unpaid time away from work and salaried managers are often pressured to forgo their leave. Given these loopholes, writes Bravo, federal government support for working families is a myth. Bravo is an advocate for women in the workforce. Since 1984 she has been an activist with 9to5, the National Association of Working Women. Currently she teaches courses on family friendly workplaces at the University of Wisconsin, Milwaukee.

As you read, consider the following questions:
1. Does the Family and Medical Leave Act apply to people who work less than twenty-five hours a week?
2. According to Bravo, what is behind teachers reporting large numbers of children coming to school sick?
3. How many hours per week does the financial company chief executive officer quoted by Bravo expect his top corporate attorney to work?

Y ou've come a long way, mama.
Consider yourself lucky this slogan doesn't grace some brand of cigarette or diaper or feminine hygiene product. Ad executives surely know that the most dramatic changes for women in the workplace have occurred among mothers. For better or worse, most moms are employed outside the home, even the majority of mothers of infants—a number the Bureau of Labor Statistics didn't even track until the mid-1970s. Employers no longer have the right to fire women for being pregnant. Mothers—and fathers—are allowed to spend time with new or seriously ill children, thanks to the Family and Medical Leave Act (FMLA).

Myth: All Women Have Maternity Leave

That's the good news. The bad news is this hard-won legal protection has loopholes large enough for a pregnant woman to walk through sideways. Take the 1978 Pregnancy Discrimination Act. This law states that if you're expecting a baby, you can't be fired or refused a job or treated differently from other employees. So far, so good. But it doesn't require your employer to keep your job open during maternity leave. I've never understood how giving away your job fails to qualify as firing you—but remember, we live in a world where the highest court once ruled that pregnancy has nothing to do with sex. If your employer offers temporary disability insurance, the policy must treat pregnancy the same as other short-term disabilities. In other words, if a coworker gets paid time off when his gall bladder is removed, you're entitled to the same benefits when you deliver a baby. That's a step forward from the days when pregnancy was excluded as a disability along with injuries that were "willfully self-inflicted or incurred during the perpetration of a high misdemeanor." But it doesn't help the majority of women who work for firms with no short-term disability policies to begin with. And not all employers gave it willingly. In the mid-1980s, when Sheila Ashley was a captain in the army, her superior officer tried to limit her maternity leave to four weeks instead of six. "He said women are getting pregnant for those six weeks of leave," she told me. "Like six weeks off makes up for a lifetime of parenthood."

Some of the problem was addressed in 1993 with passage of the Family and Medical Leave Act. Thanks to this law, not only does your employer have to allow you to take time off to have a baby, you also have the right to return from leave to the same or equivalent job. But here's the fine print: In order to qualify under the law, you must work for a firm of more than 50 employees, have been on the job for at least a year, and work there more than 25 hours a week. As a result, more than two in five private sector workers aren't covered. And many of those who are covered can't afford to take the leave because it's unpaid. Others work for employers who simply break the law—like the woman whose boss looked at her in her eighth month of pregnancy and said, "I was going to put you in charge of the office, but look at you now." Or the pregnant employee whose manager was ordered to fire her for wearing flat shoes and needing to sit down occasionally—even though she worked in a maternity clothing store. When the

Lack of Paid Parental Leave Hurts the US Economy

Millions of US workers—including parents of infants—are harmed by weak or nonexistent laws on paid leave, breastfeeding accommodation, and discrimination against workers with family responsibilities, Human Rights Watch said in a report released today [February 23, 2011]. Workers face grave health, financial, and career repercussions as a result. US employers miss productivity gains and turnover savings that these cost-effective policies generate in other countries. . . .

Parents said that having scarce or no paid leave contributed to delaying babies' immunizations, postpartum depression and other health problems, and caused mothers to give up breastfeeding early. Many who took unpaid leave went into debt and some were forced to seek public assistance. Some women said employer bias against working mothers derailed their careers. Same-sex parents were often denied even unpaid leave.

"We can't afford not to guarantee paid family leave under law—especially in these tough economic times," said Janet Walsh, deputy women's rights director at Human Rights Watch and author of the report. "The US is actually missing out by failing to ensure that all workers have access to paid family leave. Countries that have these programs show productivity gains, reduced turnover costs, and health care savings."

"US: Lack of Paid Leave Harms Workers, Children," Human Rights Watch, *February 23, 2011.*

manager failed to carry out the order, she was fired along with the subordinate.

Myth: Most Workers Can Take Time to Care for Sick Family Members

The FMLA has other limitations. Family is narrowly defined. When I served on the bipartisan Commission on Leave, appointed by Congress in 1994 to evaluate the impact of this law on employers and employees, a woman testifying at one of our hearings thanked us for allowing her to spend time with her brother when he was dying of AIDS. "Thank your employer," I told her during the break. The law doesn't include siblings—or domestic partners, grandparents, in-laws, or any other relative besides children, spouse, and parents.

Think of Rosemary, for example. Her desk has no picture of her longtime partner, Louise, because Rosemary works for an employer who could and would fire her if he knew she were a lesbian. What's worse in Rosemary's view is that she couldn't take off when Louise had breast cancer surgery. "I'd have used vacation days," she said, "but we have to give advance notice and the cancer just wasn't considerate enough to warn us." Rosemary did use vacation days to accompany Louise to most of her chemotherapy sessions—"a helluva vacation," she added.

That's another shortcoming of the FMLA—it applies only to "serious illness." Fortunately, not all children get leukemia—but they do all get the flu and ear infections, which are not covered. From time to time, children need their parents to be at school for a conference or play or sporting event; they have routine doctor appointments; they must be immunized or school won't admit them. Yet the law provides time off for none of these events. For low-wage workers, three-fourths of whom lack paid sick days, taking a day to be with a sick child can mean not only losing your wages but facing disciplinary action as well. The results? Teachers we interviewed say they've never seen so many kids coming to school sick because their parents can't take time off from work. As for their parents, many are like Judy, a factory worker in northern Wisconsin, who told me, "I go to work when I'm sick or in pain." As for doctor or dental appointments for herself or her kids? "We don't go, or I use my vacation."

Myth: The Workplace Is Family Friendly

Even when workers have the right and the means to take time off, corporate culture pressures them not to. We're deluged with commercials for cold and flu treatments that tell you how to make it to work when you're sick. Men who take more than the occasional day or week of vacation when a new baby is born are badgered about whether they're really writing a novel. "What are [you] doing, breastfeeding that baby yourself?" demanded a friend's supervisor after this new father had been off (using vacation time) for one week.

The problem has even made its way into popular culture. If you have young children or take many long flights, you may have seen the movie *Home Alone 3*. In this one, the boy comes down with chickenpox. His mother is caring for him when the boss calls to demand she come in for a meeting. "Thanks for making me choose between making the house payment and taking care of my child," she says. Regretfully she informs her son he'll have to stay home alone for a while. "But, Mom," he pleads, "what about the Family Leave Act?" The law's on his side—but the boss isn't.

Adding to the culture problem is the lack of training and accountability for many supervisors. A few years ago, the vice president of a large retail corporation came to see me. She was drafting a memo from the CEO to managers about how they sabotaged the company's leave policies. Here's the gist of the memo: "When our people ask you about leave policies, you tell them what's available—but then you add, 'Boy, will you be sorry if you use them.' They hear only the second message." Alas, this enlightened CEO (not to mention his female VP), whose memo went on to require an end to these tactics, stands among the exceptions. More common are examples cited by work-life consultants, such as the CEO at a dot-com company who, when asked about instituting concierge services to handle dry cleaning and take-out food, replied: "Anything that will glue these people to their desk for an extra hour is worth its weight in gold." Responding to a survey about flexible schedules, a financial company CEO summed up his enthusiastic support: "My chief in-house counsel [attorney] has lots of flexibility. She can work her 80 hours any way she wants."

Top Executives in Denial

Indeed, most of Corporate America continues to function as if all employees were still men with wives at home full time. Faith Wohl, formerly work-family manager at DuPont, described a senior finance executive who balked when she met with him to explain the company's new work-life policies. "I don't believe your statistics," he said, referring to numbers that showed the majority of DuPont's employees are in dual-earner couples. Wohl pointed out that he made his living working with numbers. "Yes," he said, "but no one in my neighborhood, my church, or my circle of friends has a wife who works outside the home. How could it be true of the majority of our employees?" If you think your world is *the* world and you're a top decision-maker, your front-line workers are in for a heap of trouble.

> "Middle-class breadwinners need
> assurance that they will not lose their
> jobs when they need to pick up a sick
> child or care for an ailing elder."

Programs Supporting Working Families Will Boost the Economy

Heather Boushey and Joan C. Williams

The authors of the following viewpoint argue that strengthening policies designed to support working parents balance their jobs and families will help the overall economy. Pointing out that in difficult economic conditions saving a job is as good as creating one, Heather Boushey and Joan C. Williams argue that requiring businesses to pay for family leave and to be more flexible with working hours will keep people from losing jobs when illness strikes. Such legislation already has strong support among voters of all political persuasions. Boushey is a senior economist at the Center for Economic and Policy Research and co-author of Hardships in America: The Real Story of Working Families. *Williams teaches law at the University of California's Hastings College of Law. Her most recent book is* Reshaping The Work-Family Debate: Men and Class Matter.

As you read, consider the following questions:
1. What are some of the policies touted by the authors that will help people with jobs stay employed?
2. What percentage of conservatives, moderates, and liberals (respectively) believe that mandatory paid family and medical leave should be instituted?
3. How does the percentage of stay-at-home parent households compare with those headed by working adults—meaning either single adults or two-earner couples?

A cknowledging and addressing work-family conflict is an effective way for progressives to address the economic anxieties of the broad middle class in America pragmatically and effectively. These work-life conflicts often leave Americans in the impossible position of having to choose between supporting their families or caring for them. Employers, too, face difficult decisions—ones that based on today's workplace rules are often counterproductive to their companies' bottom lines and to stronger jobs growth.

Families today are experiencing heightened economic anxiety due to the Great Recession, a slow economic recovery, and long-term structural changes in our nation's economy that are coming home to roost all at once. Creating more jobs is a key way to reduce this anxiety, but the [President Barack Obama] administration and Congress also need to address the longstanding underlying issue that is stressing families—how to provide care for loved ones when most families need all adults in the labor force and consequently have no one at home full time.

Over the past few decades, women moved into paid employment and out of the home, but our businesses and government have yet to adapt to this new reality. Family breadwinners need jobs, but they need employers to provide enough flexibility to ensure that holding a good job does not mean being unable to

San Francisco Family Leave Law Supported by Employers

As a result of the San Francisco Paid Sick Leave Ordinance (PSLO) enacted in 2007, 17 percent of San Francisco's workforce (59,000 employees) are newly covered. Under the PSLO, any part- or full-time employee who works in San Francisco—even for a company that is based elsewhere—earns one hour of paid sick time for every thirty hours worked.

Surveys of over 700 employers and nearly 1,200 employees found that two-thirds of employers support the law. Only one in seven employers reported adverse effects on profitability.

Caroline Dobuzinskis, "New Report: San Francisco Paid Sick Days Legislation Benefits Employers and Employees," Institute for Women's Policy Research, *February 10, 2011.*

be a good partner or parent or to cope with caring for an ailing family member.

No doubt you'll hear conservatives arguing that with so many out of work, now is not the time to focus on extra "perks" or "benefits" in the workplace. But now is precisely the time to address work-family conflicts because this is not about perks and benefits, but rather about jobs, future economic growth, and the family realities of the 21st century. Making sure no worker is laid off due to a child care emergency or the need to take an afternoon off to help an ailing relative will go a long way toward easing families' concerns about keeping the jobs they have.

None of this will be easy, as we'll demonstrate in our analysis below, but much of it can begin now and will reap dividends for families, businesses, and our economy in the decade ahead.

Improved Work-Family Policies
Would Have Immediate Effect

The middle class is struggling not just with job losses but also with widespread anxiety about job stability. With so many Americans out of work, families are worried that their jobs will be next on the chopping block. The challenge for the 9 in 10 workers who still have a job is how to keep it. Middle-class breadwinners need assurance that they will not lose their jobs when they need to pick up a sick child or care for an ailing elder. Addressing work-family conflict is a crucial component of an agenda to address the middle class's urgent economic concerns.

One of the challenges facing the administration is that the Great Recession was so deep and protracted. Economists agree that getting back to something like full employment may take years. Our economy would have to add nearly 250,000 jobs each and every month for the next three years just to gain back the jobs lost during the recession. Unfortunately, economists may be the only ones who find compelling the argument that the $787 billion American Recovery and Reinvestment Act made things "less bad than they could be." For families deeply concerned about job security, that is a hard sell. The American people want to see action now to address their economic anxieties.

It is true, however, especially in these tough economic times, that a job saved is as good as a job created. Policies to address work–family conflict can help those with jobs keep them, among them:

- Short-term and extended leaves from work, including paid time off for family and medical leave and paid sick days
- Workplace flexibility to allow families to plan their work lives and their family lives
- High-quality and affordable child care so that breadwinners can concentrate on work at work
- Freedom from discrimination based on family responsibilities

This is a compelling progressive policy agenda for families struggling in an economy beset with high unemployment.

Addressing Work-Family Conflict Has Mass Appeal

There is a broad base of support for policies to address work-family conflict. Recent polling commissioned by the Center for American Progress and California First Lady Maria Shriver found a widespread appetite—among men as well as women—for government and business to address the reality of families without full-time caregivers. This poll, conducted by The Rockefeller Foundation and Time, Inc., surveyed more than 3,400 adults across the country in early September 2009 and found that overwhelming majorities of both men and women said that government and businesses need to provide flexible work schedules, better child care, and paid family and medical leave.

A full 85 percent of Americans agree that businesses that fail to adapt to the needs of modern families risk losing good workers, and 75 percent agree that employers should be required to give workers more flexibility. But the appetite for change is also broad based:

- Sixty-four percent of conservatives and 81 percent of moderates join the 89 percent of liberals who believe that businesses should be required to provide paid family and medical leave for every worker who needs it.
- Sixty-five percent of conservatives and 80 percent of moderates join the 85 percent of liberals who believe that employers should be required to give workers more workplace flexibility.
- Fifty percent of conservatives and 75 percent of moderates join the 85 percent of liberals who believe that the government should provide more funding for child care.

Also notable is that these kinds of "family-friendly" policies also find support among Americans who have traditionally supported a family values agenda, such as evangelicals. Among evangelical Christians, 74 percent believe that businesses should be required to provide paid family and medical leave for every worker who needs it, 71 percent believe that employers should be required to give workers more flexibility in work schedules, and 66 percent believe that the government should provide more funding for child care. This strong support for government programs among voters who otherwise trend conservative highlights the powerful potential of work-family issues to help meld a progressive coalition.

Work-Family Conflict: Not Just for Women

One of the key facts about work-family conflict is it's not just about women. Men now report higher levels of work-family conflict than women. We think that this may be because the typical man no longer has a stay-at-home wife and he—and she—are sharing the responsibilities (and joys!) of working outside the home and caring for family members. While some men struggle with the rise of women in the workplace, most have accepted, if not embraced, this new way of living.

Addressing work-family conflict is not a frill for women, but rather a necessary policy agenda for all workers and their families. In two-thirds of families, mothers are either breadwinners or co-breadwinners. Few families have the luxury of an adult at home full time to provide care for children or ailing family members.

Families are three times as likely to be headed by working adults—either a single, working parent (22 percent) or a two-job couple (44 percent)—as they are to have a stay-at-home wife (21 percent). The problem is that men and women remain concerned about who's caring for the children and other family members. Helping these breadwinners work more effectively and care for their families more consistently builds better businesses and better communities for the common good. . . .

Progressive Solutions to
Work-Family Issues

The Obama administration recognizes that addressing work-family conflict is crucial to supporting middle-class families and to tackling the long-term challenges facing our economy and society. In the first annual report of Vice President Biden's Middle Class Task Force, the administration reiterated that creating good jobs is critical to middle-class families' economic stability. But the report also addressed long-term economic challenges that predate the Great Recession—challenges that include balancing work and family needs as our economy recovers and finding new avenues of growth alongside the more traditional issues of college access and affordability, and retirement security.

The findings of the vice president's task force are evident in the administration's fiscal year 2011 budget, which:

- More than doubles the Child and Dependent Care Tax Credit, helping most families with incomes below $115,000

- Provides the largest one-year increase ever ($1.6 billion) in funding for child care programs for low-income children

- Establishes a $50 million State Paid Leave Fund to move toward remedying the fact that the United States is the only country among the top 30 industrialized democracies in the in the world that lacks paid maternity leave.

In short, addressing work-family conflict demonstrates to Americans that progressive government policies can help workers and families help themselves and the broader economy recover and grow more competitive. Matching the 21st century workplace to the needs of the 21st century workforce is a crucial progressive goal.

> "The ultimate goal is for organizations to view the issues brought on by an increasingly diverse workforce not as marginal problems but as opportunities for productive change."

Family-Friendly Measures Can Improve Worker Productivity

Lotte Bailyn

The following viewpoint presents the case for more flexible hours, arguing that flexibility can increase worker productivity. Using two examples, one from the customer service division of an unnamed company, and the other from the well-known electronics and appliance retailer Best Buy, the author, Lotte Bailyn, shows that when given more control over their work schedules, employees manage to coordinate among themselves, improving both their productivity and their ability to meet family obligations. The author also makes the case that skills learned in managing family affairs can help workers be more effective in the new, more flexible work environments. Bailyn is a professor of management at the Massachusetts Institute of Technology's Sloan School of Management and a pioneer researcher in the study of work-family balance. Her book, Breaking the Mold: Redesigning Work for Productive and Satisfying Lives, *was first published in 1993 and, with significant revisions, again in 2006.*

As you read, consider the following questions:
1. Why, during the three-month experiment with flexible scheduling at the customer service unit, was it necessary to have employees coordinate schedules among themselves?
2. What were some specific results of the three-month flexible schedule experiment?
3. How much did job satisfaction increase at Best Buy when they instituted flexible scheduling?

In organizations built on the acceptance of equal legitimacy of the needs of work and of workers' personal lives, employees would take responsibility for high-quality and timely work. They would arrange individually or within teams for the appropriate allocation of assignments, time schedules, and location of work to guarantee this result. Companies in turn would "reengineer" the work process to ensure that demands on workers reflect only the basic requirements for reaching organizational goals.

Problems with Schedules

An example of how such a collective, more systemic view benefits both employees and the company comes from [a] customer service division. . . . The three hundred or so employees of this unit, under the direction of a controller, were engaged in phone contacts with customers about scheduling, billing, and other routine concerns. Since customer satisfaction was a key component of the organization's goals, this direct-contact unit played a significant role. The employees were divided into groups, each with a supervisor, who reported to a middle level of management before reaching the controller. The controller was a careful leader. He seldom embarked on changes until they had been shown to work elsewhere or unless they were handed down from corporate headquarters. Nonetheless, there were some problems in the unit. In particular, the controller was concerned about absenteeism, which was running very high. And there were sanctions for lateness, which was always noted. When we began working with his unit, they were waiting for empowerment training to arrive from corporate headquarters. There had been a move in the company toward self-managed work groups, and they had established quite an elaborate training to help this process along.

The company had progressive work-family policies. Every flexibility imaginable (e.g., job sharing, four-day workweeks, flexible starting and ending times) was on the books. But not much was being used in this unit. An occasional employee was allowed slight deviation of starting and ending time, but there were no compressed workweeks and no job sharing. The latter, though, was not of great concern because this was not a high-paying job, and few employees could have afforded less than full-time work. Each request to use one of these flexibilities had to be carefully documented by the employee and approved by his or her supervisor. Since supervisors felt that they needed to be present whenever their subordinates were, it was not surprising that there was little deviation from the traditional nine-to-five workday.

The division was in an urban area, and many employees had difficult commutes. A number had children to bring to day care each morning or other responsibilities that could not always be met on weekends. Though the supervisors seemed mainly to consider the needs of mothers when giving their permissions, these were not the only ones to want flexible arrangements. What generally happened was that an employee would ask for an alternative schedule, be turned down, word would spread, and soon fewer and fewer employees submitted requests. This only confirmed management's view that such flexibilities were not really necessary. When the controller realized that these self-reinforcing rigidities were rampant in his organization, and not confined only to family benefits, he became willing to set up an experiment.

Workers Have Limited Access to the Flexibility They Need for Family Life

- Flexible work schedules are available to less than one-third of workers nationally.

- 27.4 million, or 27.5%, of all full-time wage and salary workers have access to flexible work schedules according to federal surveys of employers.

- Despite increasing numbers of women and mothers in the workforce, less than one quarter (22%) report that their work schedule suits their child or elder caring needs.

- Other flexible work arrangements important to families, like job-sharing and telecommuting, are also not widely available.

- According to the Family and Work Institute's National Study of Employers, 44% of companies allowed *some* employees to share jobs. However, only 13% of companies allowed *all* or *most* employees to share jobs.

- In the same survey, 31% of organizations allowed some employees to work at home or off-site on a regular basis; only 3% allowed this for *all* or most employees.

"Meeting the Needs of Today's Families,"
Workplace Flexibility 2010
Congressional Briefing, May 2006.
www.workplaceflexibility2010.org.

A Radical Experiment

One day, before the entire unit, he said he would let anyone take advantage of any of the alternative work arrangements they wanted as long as the work got done. It could last for three months and then they would evaluate. So what happened? First, almost everyone—men and women, parents and nonparents—wanted a different schedule. Second, with this increased number of requests, the supervisors were no longer able to negotiate these changes one-on-one with each employee. They had no choice but to let the groups get together and figure out their schedules collectively to ensure that the work would get done. And, since schedules now roamed much more broadly over the day, supervisors had to let employees work at times without their presence.

And what were the results for the company? Absenteeism decreased by 30 percent. Customer service, which had been a great concern, improved because more hours of the day were now being covered. And once the groups found they could manage their own schedules, they began to take over some of the self-management tasks (such as coordinating the work and making hiring decisions) that had been envisioned for them, but which had stalled, waiting for the arrival of corporate training. The groups developed so well that when corporate training finally arrived, they sent it back, feeling they were way ahead of the game. Perhaps most important, the controller changed his image of himself. He now saw himself as innovative and experimental rather than as conservative.

So what happened here? We see willingness, mandated by top management, to put personal needs up front, though under the constraint that the work must get done and within a strict experimental framework. To meet this double goal—flexible schedules for employees combined with work effectiveness—a number of things happened. First, everyone was empowered to ask for the schedule he or she needed to get their work done, and hence absenteeism dropped dramatically. Second, negotiation on schedules no longer could be done one-on-one between employee and supervisor, hence the groups had to deal with schedules collectively. This enabled them, over time, to become the self-managed teams that had been envisioned for them but which had seemed so difficult to bring about.

A key assumption about control was challenged by this change. Supervisors were forced to relinquish the notion that they had to be there whenever their subordinates were, and thus learned that surveillance may not be the best way to manage people. Of course, they could have been told this, but they had to experience it to change their assumptions about control. . . .

Starting with people's work schedules leads to changes in the way the work is being done and managed, which increases the commitment of employees and thus has positive effects for both the organization and the people involved. And since the flexibilities were available to everyone, both equity and effectiveness were served.

Productive Change

The ultimate goal is for organizations to view the issues brought on by an increasingly diverse workforce not as marginal problems but as opportunities for productive change in the organization of work. Companies need not embark on this path only for the common good; on the contrary, by being innovative in their response to employee needs, they necessarily have to rethink their accepted ways of doing work. Such an effort is likely to produce greater long-run productivity, as well as to enhance the overall commitment and responsibility of employees toward the organization's goals.

Take the example of [electronics and appliance retailer] Best Buy. For three years [2003–2006] they have been running an experiment in a number of divisions (voluntary on the part of the participating groups) that they call ROWE (results-oriented work environment). It started with one troubled retail group and an HR representative who suggested that the manager try flexible scheduling and trust the group to do it. The manager agreed, and the group of about three hundred employees, as in the example above, collectively designed their schedules. The results were dramatic: "Turnover in the first three months of employment fell from 14% to zero, job satisfaction rose 10%, and their team-performance scores rose 13%." This result led the company to offer ROWE to any group or division that wanted to try, but it must be done by agreement of a whole group—never by an individual. Each group finds its own way to manage the various and often unpredictable schedules of its employees and to deal with the extensive changes in assumptions and attitudes that the experiment entails. On the whole, the experiments are successful, though there are searching questions that remain: Single people who made their mark by long hours at the office fret how they will be recognized; managers worry how to establish authority in this system; employees sometimes miss the structure of the traditional nine-to-five day. Best Buy addresses these lingering attitudes through what they call "sludge sessions." Groups in ROWE are trained to cry "sludge" whenever someone makes a comment based on the old assumptions, as for example indicating surprise when someone comes late or leaves early.

Personal Skills Improve Work Productivity

Allowing employees to integrate their paid work with personal involvements may also have less obvious positive consequences. . . . Might there not be attributes acquired in personal life that could be usefully applied to the occupational world? One working mother, for example—a director in the financial division of a large consumer products corporation—reported that "as an outgrowth of being a mother and having household responsibilities, I learned how to do things faster, [to] organize my time for things that have to be done, [and] to constantly reevaluate the priorities and plan ahead." These organizational skills, learned in her home, allowed her to be a valuable employee even though she put strict limits on her office presence.

Other skills could also transfer from private life to the accomplishment of organizational work. American companies are concerned about the lack of skills in the workforce to ensure coordinated, team-oriented, interactive, and interdependent ways of working. But many of these same employees display these skills in their private lives. For example, a 2005 article in the *Harvard Business Review* chides companies for not taking advantage of the skills learned by their minority professionals in the many leadership roles they hold in their communities and churches. Perhaps if companies valued this aspect of their employees' lives more fully, they would find such skills being used in occupational work. And perhaps by expecting employee time and energy to be applied primarily in the workplace, they are preventing the development of the very skills they say they need.

> *"One review identified that not all flexible family-friendly policies uniformly improved productivity and some, such as job-sharing, actually decreased productivity."*

Results of Work-Life Balance Polices Are Mixed

Paula Brough et al.

In this viewpoint, Paula Brough and her team analyze several studies of the implementation of work-life balance policies. Nations and companies recognize the importance of restructuring work in the face of declining family size and aging populations. An often heard solution to these challenges is to give workers more flexible schedules and the opportunity to take time off to attend to family matters. However the results of such work-life balance policies have so far been mixed. The "breadwinner model," in which one member of the family (usually the man) works a full-time job and earns most of the income, has persisted. This has slowed the adoption of scheduling innovations in the workplace. Where they are tried, they are often only partially implemented. Businesses have cause to be cautious, as some new models of work scheduling have been

Paula Brough, Jackie Holt, Rosie Bauld, Amanda Biggs, and Claire Ryan, "The Ability of Work-Life Balance Policies to Influence Key Social/Organisational Issues," *Asia Pacific Journal of Human Resources*, SAGE publications, copyright Australian Human Resources Institute, vol. 46, no. 3, 2008. Copyright © 2008 by SAGE Publications. All rights reserved. Reproduced by permission of SAGE.

shown to decrease productivity. The authors conclude that further developments are needed to ensure continued progress toward an ideal work-life balance. Brough is an organizational psychologist whose main research interest is occupational psychological health. She led a doctoral researcher and several student doctoral candidates to produce the research for the viewpoint that follows.

As you read, consider the following questions:

1. How much did US organizations pay in 2006 for discrimination against pregnant employees, as reported in this viewpoint?
2. According to economists Bloom, Kretchmer, and Van Reenen, what two problems do businesses face when trying to implement work-life balance policies?
3. What are some negative consequences found to be associated with part-time work, according to the authors of this viewpoint?

Over the past 25 years many industrialised nations have undergone economic reform marked by increases in downsizing, work intensification, unpaid overtime, and expectations for higher employee performance. Approximately half of the overtime worked in Australia is unpaid due to understaffing. . . .

Key Issues Facing Organisations

Organisations are adversely impacted by work-life conflict through reductions in productivity and increased withdrawal (i.e. absenteeism, turnover) of employees. Some of these adverse consequences may be mitigated by the provision of useable family-friendly policies. Work-life balance and family–friendly policies are usually regarded only in positive terms; they have been heralded as strategies that organisations can implement to recruit and retain staff, as well as to decrease absenteeism and levels of occupational stress Family-friendly policies are also positively perceived by shareholders, and organisations that have announced work-life balance initiatives have typically observed a (short-term) increase in their share price. However, the actual *cost-effectiveness* of these policies and their genuine ability to promote work-life balance requires further exploration.

Both the individual and organisational consequences of overwork and occupational stress have been identified and include high levels of employee sickness absences and decreased job performance. Similarly, failure by organisations to address issues of work-life balance and to prevent discrimination towards pregnant employees can result in considerable organisational costs via high levels of employee absenteeism, turnover, and compensation claims. The organisational costs associated with absenteeism occurring specifically as a result of role overload and work-life imbalance were estimated at approximately 11 [Canadian dollars] billion per year. Similarly, the turnover of skilled workers who leave the workforce due to insufficient work-life balance has been estimated to cost British organisations approximately 126 million [British Pounds] per year. The voluntary turnover of female staff is associated with the absence of accessible family-friendly programs, a non-supportive supervisor, and an unsupportive workplace culture. Finally, the consequences arising from maternity and pregnancy discrimination are also relevant. In the US in 2006 approximately 10.4 million [US dollars] was paid by organisations for pregnancy discrimination alone.

Work-Life Balance and Family-Friendly Policies

There is mixed evidence regarding the cost-effectiveness of work-life balance and family-friendly policies. Some research links these policies with reduced levels of employee turnover, increased employee satisfaction, commitment and productivity, and decreased rates of physical and emotional disorders associated with work-life conflict. [Sociologists Jennifer] Glass and

[Lisa] Riley demonstrated that a positive relationship existed between the provision of adequate maternity leave and reduced rates of turnover in US female employees. Similarly, Australian research found that 70% of businesses that incorporated telework options reported a number of positive benefits, such as increased business productivity and reduced costs, improved employee flexibility and work-life balance, and increased workforce participation. This research also reported that the major barriers to telework were unsupportive organisational culture and management practices, rather than technological barriers.

However, research has also identified an *increase* in organisational costs due to work-life balance policies. One review identified that not all flexible family-friendly policies uniformly improved productivity and some, such as job-sharing, actually *decreased* productivity. In addition, some researchers have questioned whether the cost of implementing work-family balance policies is commensurate with subsequent gains in productivity.

> [Economists Nick] Bloom, [Tobias] Kretchmer, and [John] Van Reenen argued: Improving work-life balance is socially desirable—workers obviously like it and Firm productivity does not suffer. However, our results do not give a green light for policy makers to regulate even more work-life balance. Even if productivity does not fall, work-life balance is costly to implement and maintain, and may result in significantly lower profitability.

Similarly, a recent comprehensive study of 2191 UK organisations found that the organisational costs of family-friendly policies were offset by reduced employee earnings. . . .

Thus, it appears that family-friendly and work-life balance initiatives *can* support organisations to address key issues such as retention and productivity. However, specific organisational and legislative conditions should be considered to ensure that the implementation of work-life balance policies have long-term positive outcomes for both employees and organisations.

The presence of formal and informal 'barriers' often restrict (or block) employee access to work-life balance policies. Examples of such barriers include supervisor support, co-worker attitudes, perceived negative career consequences, and societal norms. This 'provision-utilisation gap' of work-life balance employment policies is now recognised as a pertinent research issue.

Further Developments Are Needed

This paper has briefly reviewed some of the issues facing industrialised nations in regards to work-life balance employment initiatives. We have argued that recent changes in employment practices and social developments ensure that work-life balance is a pertinent economic and social issue, with ramifications for the labour market, healthcare costs, and the ageing population. Despite some movement away from the traditional 'breadwinner model' many jobs have not been redesigned to make provisions for non-work responsibilities. In fact, while there has been a proliferation of work-life and family-friendly policies, there have been few real attempts to reorganise workplaces to ensure such policies can be effectively applied. In most industrialised nations, there remains a predominance of men in full-time employment, while women bear the majority of child-rearing and household responsibilities. While some individuals freely choose this arrangement, others have limited choice. The emergence of part-time work, especially within Australia, was feted as a legitimate way in which workers with dependants could achieve a successful work-life balance. However, part-time work is also associated with a range of negative consequences including a reinforcement of the traditional male model of work, decreased career aspirations, decreased security and income for women (especially within the context of changing family dynamics), and *lower* levels of work-life balance. We acknowledge that effective work-life balance policies require examination from a broad perspective. There is considerable variance between countries and the degree to which their governments are involved in the reconciliation of work and non-work responsibilities. Legal and industrial relations developments are needed to ensure that work-life balance policies and practices are not only provided but are also actually accessible and used by employees.

> *"Today's family has no margin for error. There is no leeway to cut back if one earner's hours are cut or if the other gets sick."*

Necessity of Having Two Incomes Puts Families at Financial Risk

Elizabeth Warren

The following viewpoint lays out Elizabeth Warren's case that middle-class families today are at financial risk. Due to the second income brought in by working women, households have larger incomes (on average) than families a generation ago. Despite this, they have less disposable income. The main reasons for the paradox are increases in mortgage and healthcare costs as well as higher taxes. In addition having a second earner in the workforce means new expenses such as childcare and transportation for the second worker. The result is that today's working and middle-class families have less discretionary income than their counterparts a generation ago. They are also at greater risk—if one earner gets laid off or becomes seriously ill, the typical family will have difficulty cutting back enough to meet the core household expenses of mortgage, food, and health insurance. Warren is a professor of law at Har-

vard Law School and the author of the Two-Income Trap: Why Middle-Class Mothers and Fathers Are Going Broke. *She also serves as special advisor to the United States Treasury Secretary, consulting on the Consumer Financial Protection Bureau.*

As you read, consider the following questions:

1. What percentage of working mothers report that they have a job to support their families?
2. What percentage of family income went to taxes in the early 1970s and how does that compare with the taxes paid in the early 2000s?
3. How much of today's household income goes to recurrent monthly expenses such as the mortgage and utilities?

Why are so many moms in the workforce? For some it is the lure of a great job, but for millions more, it is the need for a paycheck, plain and simple. Incomes for men are flat at a time when expenses are rising sharply. Fully 80% of working mothers report that their main reason for working was to support their families. In short, families now put two people in the workforce to do what one could accomplish alone just a generation ago.

It would be convenient to blame the families and say that it is their lust for stuff that has gotten them into this mess. Indeed, there are those who do exactly that. Sociologist Robert Frank claims that America's newfound "Luxury Fever" forces middle-class families "to finance their consumption increases largely by reduced savings and increased debt." Others echo the theme. A book titled *Affluenza* sums it up: "The dogged pursuit for more" accounts for Americans' "overload, debt, anxiety, and waste." If Americans are out of money, it must be because they are over-consuming, buying junk they don't really need.

Blaming the family supposes that we believe that families spend their money on things they don't really need. Over-consumption is not about medical care or basic housing; it is, in the words of Juliet Schor, about "designer clothes, a microwave, restaurant meals, home and automobile air conditioning, and, of course, Michael Jordan's ubiquitous athletic shoes, about which children and adults both display near-obsession." And it isn't about buying a few goodies with extra income; it is about going deep into debt to finance consumer purchases that sensible people could do without.

But is it true? Intuitions and anecdotes are no substitute for hard data. If families really are blowing their paychecks on designer clothes and restaurant meals, then the expenditure data should show that today's families are spending more on these frivolous items than ever before. But the numbers don't back up the claim. . . .

Most Spending Is on Basics

So where did their money go? It went to the basics. The real increases in family spending are for the items that make a family middle class and keep them safe (housing, health insurance), and that let them earn a living (transportation, child care and taxes).

The data can be summarized in a financial snapshot of two families, a typical one-earner family from the early 1970s compared with a typical two-earner family from the early 2000s. With an income of $42,450 (all 1970s numbers are inflation adjusted), the average family from the early 1970s covered their basic mortgage expenses of $5,820, health insurance costs of $1,130 and car payments, maintenance, gas, and repairs of $5,640. Taxes claimed about 24 percent of their income, leaving them with $19,560 in discretionary income. That means they had about $1,500 a month to cover food, clothing, utilities, and anything else they might need—just about half of their income.

By 2004, the family budget looks very different. . . . While a man is making nearly $800 less than his counterpart a generation ago, his wife's paycheck brings the family to a combined income that is $73,770—a 75% increase. But their expenses quickly re-

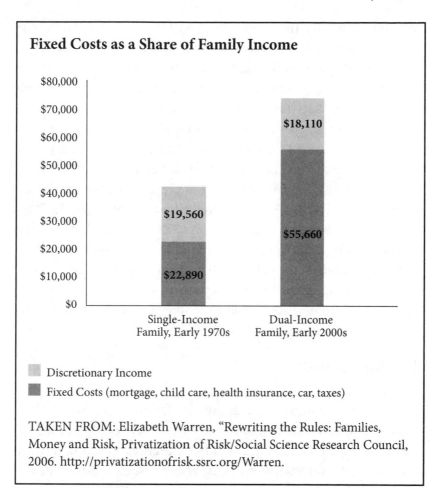

Fixed Costs as a Share of Family Income

- Discretionary Income
- Fixed Costs (mortgage, child care, health insurance, car, taxes)

TAKEN FROM: Elizabeth Warren, "Rewriting the Rules: Families, Money and Risk, Privatization of Risk/Social Science Research Council, 2006. http://privatizationofrisk.ssrc.org/Warren.

verse that bit of good financial news. Their annual mortgage payments are more than $10,500. If they have a child in elementary school who goes to daycare after school and in the summers, the family will spend $5,660. If their second child is a pre-schooler, the cost is even higher, $6,920 a year. With both people in the workforce, the family spends more than $8,000 a year on its two vehicles. Health insurance costs the family $1,970, and taxes now take 30 percent of the family's money.

The bottom line: today's median earning, median spending middle class family sends two people into the workforce, but at the end of the day they have about $1,500 *less* for discretionary spending than their one-income counterparts of a generation ago.

What happens to the family that tries to get by on a single income in today's economy? Their expenses would be a little lower because they can save on child care and taxes, and, if they are lucky enough to live close to shopping and other services, perhaps they can get by without a second car. But if they tried to live a normal, middle-class life in other ways—buy an average home, send their younger child to preschool, purchase health insurance, and so forth—they would be left with only $5,500 a year to cover all their other expenses. They would have to find a way to buy food, clothing, utilities, life insurance, furniture, appliances, and so on with less than $500 a month. The modern single-earner family trying to keep up an average lifestyle faces a 72 *percent* drop in discretionary income compared with its one-income counterpart of a generation ago.

Families at Risk

But the biggest change has been on the risk front. In the early 1970s, if any calamity came along, the family had nearly half its income in discretionary spending. Of course, people need to eat and turn on the lights, but the other expenses—clothing, furniture, appliances, restaurant meals, vacations, entertainment and pretty much everything else—can be drastically reduced or even cut out entirely. In other words, they didn't need as much money if something went wrong. If they could find a way through unemployment insurance, savings or putting their stay-at-home parent to work, they could cover the basics on just 50% of their previous earnings. Because of the option of a second paycheck, both could stay in the workforce for a few months once the crisis had passed, and pull out of their financial hole.

But today's family is in a very different position. Fully 75 percent of their income is earmarked for recurrent monthly expenses. Even if they are able to trim around the edges, families are faced with a sobering truth: Every one of those expensive items

we identified—mortgage, car payments, insurance, tuition—
is a fixed cost. Families must pay them each and every month,
through good times and bad times, no matter what. Unlike
clothing or food, there is no way to cut back from one month
to the next. Short of moving out of the house, withdrawing their
children from preschool, or canceling the insurance policy altogether, they are stuck.

Today's family has no margin for error. There is no leeway
to cut back if one earner's hours are cut or if the other gets sick.
There is no room in the budget if someone needs to take off
work to care for a sick child or an elderly parent. The modern
American family is walking a high wire without a net. Their basic situation is far riskier than that of their parents a generation
earlier. If anything—anything at all—goes wrong, then today's
two-income family is in big trouble. . . .

What Happens to Our Middle Class?

Family by family, the middle class now faces higher risks that a
job loss or a medical problem will push them over the edge. They
are working harder than ever just to maintain a tenuous grasp
on a middle-class life. Plenty of families make it, but a growing
number of those who worked just as hard and followed the rules
just as carefully find themselves in a financial nightmare. A once-
secure middle class has disappeared. In its place are millions of
families whose grip on the good life can be shaken loose in an
instant.

> *"Because of this huge increase in the tax bite, the percentage of family income dedicated to payments for health insurance, mortgage, and automobiles actually fell between the two periods."*

High Taxes Put the Middle Class in Peril

Todd Zywicki

The following viewpoint is Todd Zywicki's critique of Elizabeth Warren and Amelia Warren Tyagi's "two-income trap" hypothesis—the idea that contemporary married couples with both spouses in the workforce are at more financial risk than the single earner couples of a generation before. For Warren and Tyagi, the desire of middle class parents to live in areas with good schools has driven up housing prices, thus creating the need for couples to earn more income to qualify for mortgage loans. Zywicki, on the other hand, shows that the biggest increase in family expenditures has been taxes, casting into doubt the idea that mortgage costs are forcing women to work. Further, he questions Warren and Tyagi's logic— he believes that household spending is not external (exogenous) to income earned, but rather internal (endogenous) to household income. That is, rather than higher housing and car costs requiring households to have two incomes, it may be that the higher income available to dual-earner couples enables greater spending on cars and houses. Zywicki is a professor of law at George Mason University. He is the author of more than thirty articles.

As you read, consider the following questions:

1. What, according to Zywicki's summary of the argument of the "two-income trap," is the single category of expenditure that is driving women into the workplace?
2. For the "typical" families in the article, how much did the 1970s family pay in taxes? How much did the 2000s family pay?
3. In contrast to Warren and Tyagi, what policy recommendation does Zywicki make to eliminate the "two-income trap?"

I've been going back through the various hypotheses that have been advanced for the rise in American bankruptcy filings in the 1980s and 1990s. One hypothesis was that advanced in *The Two-Income Trap: Why Middle Class Mothers and Fathers are Going Broke* by Professor Elizabeth Warren and Amelia Warren Tyagi.

Warren & Tyagi's argument can be easily summarized. They focus on the rise in the number of households with two parents working as an indication of economic distress. Conventional economic theory would indicate that one benefit of having a second wage-earner is that it will make the family more resilient to a financial setback or loss of job than a traditional family with only one wage-earner. Families today, unlike those a generation ago, can save the second earner's income as precautionary savings, thereby making it easier to withstand a setback.

Bucking Conventional Economics

Warren and Tyagi disagree with this conventional economic approach.

They argue that contrary to standard economic theory, the influx of a second worker has actually made a family more susceptible to economic setback. The argument is a bit opaque, but it seems to rest on the idea that recent decades have seen an excessive "bidding war" for housing, as families compete to get their children into preferred school districts. This bidding war for housing has, in turn, driven mothers from the home into the workplace, in order to earn sufficient income to pay the mortgage on high-priced homes. In turn, this increased female workforce participation has given rise to a whole new host of expenses, such as additional cars and child care expenses. In the end, Warren and Tyagi argue, the family is no more financially stable or well-off, because now both incomes are needed to pay for the house, as well as the necessary expenses associated with maintaining a two-income family, such as an additional car to get to work and daycare. Warren and Tyagi have dubbed this phenomenon the "two-income trap," which, at its core, is said to be driven by the rapid appreciation in housing prices. Because houses in good neighborhoods are expensive, thus in order to pay the mortgage, mom goes to work to supplement dad's income.

So although the second job brings in new income, it brings with it a whole new set of expenses, many of which are supposedly dedicated to sustaining mom's employment, such as child care expenses and another car. So the family ends up even more highly leveraged than previously and with a higher family income and two wage-earners, but counterintuitively, more vulnerable to financial setback than previously. . . .

Comparing 1970s and 2000s Households

Warren and Tyagi's argument rests on a stylized example of the situation facing a "typical" middle class family today versus a generation ago. All figures are inflation adjusted:

We [Warren and Tyagi] offer two examples.

We begin with Tom and Susan, representatives of the average middle-class family of a generation ago [early 1970s]. Tom works full-time, earning $38,700, the median income for a fully employed man in 1973, while Susan stays at home to care for the house and children. Tom and Susan have the typical two children, one in grade school and a three-year-old who stays home with Susan. The family buys health insurance through Tom's job, to which they contribute $1,030 a year—the average amount spent by an insured family that made at least some contribution to the cost of a private insurance policy. They own an average home in an average family neighborhood—costing them $5,310 a year in mortgage payments. Shopping is within walking distance, so the family owns just one car, on which it spends $5,140 a year for car payments, maintenance, gas, and repairs. And like all good citizens, they pay their taxes, which claim about 24 percent of Tom's income. Once all the taxes, mortgage payments, and other fixed expenses are paid, Tom and Susan are left with $17,834 in discretionary income (inflation adjusted), or about 46 percent of Tom's pretax paycheck. They aren't rich, but they have nearly $1,500 a month to cover food, clothing, utilities, and anything else they might need. So how does our 1973 couple compare with Justin and Kimberly, the modern-day version of the traditional family? Like Tom, Justin is an average earner, bringing home $39,000 in 2000—not even 1 percent more than his counterpart of a generation ago. But there is one big difference: Thanks to Kimberly's full-time salary, the family's combined income is $67,800—a whopping 75 percent higher than the household income for Tom and Susan. A quick look at their income statement shows how the modern dual-income couple has sailed past their single-income counterpart of a generation ago. So where did all that money go? Like Tom and Susan they bought an average home, but today that three-bedroom-two-bath ranch costs a lot more. Their annual mortgage payments are nearly $9,000.

The older child still goes to the public elementary school, but after school and during summer vacations he goes to day care, at an average yearly cost of $4,350. The younger child attends a full-time preschool day care program, which costs the family $5,320 a year. With Kimberly at work, the second car is a must, so the family spends more than $8,000 a year on its two vehicles. Health insurance is another must, and even with Justin's employer picking up a big share of the cost, insurance takes $1,650 from the couple's paychecks. Taxes also take their toll. Thanks in part to Kimberly's extra income, the family has been bumped into a higher bracket, and the government takes 33 percent of the family's money. So where does that leave Justin and Kimberly after these basic expenses are deducted? With $17,045—about $800 *less* than Tom and Susan, who were getting by on just one income.

Reading that excerpt, I thought, "Hmm, that's confusing. I wonder why they listed the actual dollar values for all of the other expenses, but the 'percentage' of income spent on taxes. That makes it difficult to compare to make an apples to apples comparison of the actual tax burdens between the two periods." Presenting it in this manner is even more confusing because the authors then go on to implicitly convert tax obligations to dollar values in order to calculate the total amount of the families' budgets dedicated to aggregate "fixed costs" versus "discretionary spending," concluding that the 2000s couple has less left over for discretionary spending than the prior generation. Yet, although they report the actual dollar values for everything else, in an apparent oversight, they never actually report the actual dollar figures for the tax expenditures in the two periods.

Doing the Math

So I got out my handy calculator and calculated what the indicated percentage of taxes translates into in terms of actual dollars paid in taxes. In turns out that for the 1970s family, paying 24%

of its income in taxes works out to be $9,288. And for the 2000s family, paying 33% of its income (a higher rate presumably because of progressivity hitting the second wage-earner's income) in taxes works out to be $22,374.

Thus, taxes increase in the example by $13,086. By contrast, annual mortgage obligations increased by only $3,690 and automobile obligations by $2,860 and health insurance $620. Those increases are not trivial, but they are swamped by the increase in tax obligations. To put this in perspective, the increase in tax obligations is *over three times as large as the increase in the mortgage* (the supposed driver of the "two income trap") and about double the increase in the *combined* obligations of mortgage and automobile payments. This also leaves aside the peculiarity that the 2000s family is paying $9,670 in new child care and $2,860 in new automobile expenses supposedly to meet a $3,690 increase in mortgage expenses, the supposed driver of the model.

Indeed, because of this huge increase in the tax bite, the *percentage* of family income dedicated to payments for health insurance, mortgage, and automobiles actually *fell* between the two periods. . . .

Overall, the typical family in the 2000s pays substantially more in taxes than in their mortgage, automobile, expenses, and health insurance costs combined. And the growth in the tax obligation between the two periods is substantially greater than the growth in mortgage, automobile expenses, and health insurance costs combined. And note, this is using the data taken directly from Warren and Tyagi's book.

The Tax Burden Is the Problem

It is not clear what to make of all of this, except that it is hard to see how this confirms the central hypothesis of the "two-income trap" that "necessary" expenses such as mortgage, car payments, and health insurance are the primary drain on the modern family's budget. And again, this unrealistically assumes that all increased spending on houses and cars is exogenously [externally] determined, ignoring the possibility that an increase in income leads to an endogenous [internal] decision by some households to increase their expenditures on items such as houses and cars.

Instead, Warren and Tyagi's data point to the conclusion that the obvious problem for this "typical" American family appears to be an extremely high tax burden caused primarily by the progressive nature of the income tax that hits families with two working adults by kicking them into higher marginal tax rates. . . .

Finally, this confusion about the underlying dynamic also leads to confusion about policy recommendations. In particular, although Warren and Tyagi do not make this argument, it would seem to follow that one logical policy implication of this analysis would be to support a lower and flatter marginal tax rate. This would reduce the household tax burden and increase available discretionary income.

"Demographic and societal shifts over the last 40 years have resulted in an increased and acute need for various types of workplace flexibility, including paid time off for health and caregiving reasons."

Family Security Insurance Would Ease Work and Family Challenges

Workplace Flexibility 2010/Berkeley Center on Health, Economic and Family Security

In most other industrialized countries, employers are required by law to give mothers and fathers paid leave for family matters. These leave policies are generally designed to support new parents immediately after the birth of their children, but some include leave for workers who need to take care of a sick child or elderly parent. When Australia passed a paid family leave act, the United States was left as the last economically advanced nation without mandatory, paid family-related leave. The following viewpoint is excerpted from a report jointly authored by a policy initiative of the Georgetown University Law Center and a think-tank based at the University of California at Berkeley. The authors believe that

Workplace Flexibility 2010/Berkeley Center on Health, Economic and Family Security, "Family Security Insurance—a New Foundation for Economic Security," December, 2010. Copyright © 2010 by Georgetown University Law Center. All rights reserved. Reproduced by permission.

research findings show that families need something beyond the current Family and Medical Leave Act (FMLA), which mandates only unpaid leave. The two organizations promote the concept of a comprehensive national plan on workplace flexibility, as well as guaranteed, paid time off from work for employees to care for a new child or family members with serious illness

As you read, consider the following questions:

1. In what proportion of households are women the primary or co-breadwinner?
2. According to the viewpoint, what percentage of likely voters favor extending current law to provide paid leave?
3. What are some examples of the adverse effects for children when mothers return to work soon (six weeks or less) after birth?

Over the course of our lives and careers, almost all of us will need time off from work to care for our children, our own health needs, or those of a family member. This has always been true, but the problem, magnified by demographic shifts, is now a nearly universal challenge.

Yet our national policy on paid time off from work for health and caregiving reasons has not caught up with today's reality. As a result, individuals, families, and employers are largely left to muddle through on their own, with only a patchwork of support that falls far short of the demand. This inaction has consequences not only for individuals and families, but also for business and the overall economy.

This report offers one solution to the problem of how we support ourselves, our families, our businesses, and our economy through some of life's most complex and challenging moments. It offers a blueprint for a national social insurance program—which we call "Family Security Insurance" (FSI)—to provide income replacement for workers when they are away from work

US Lags Behind Other Countries in Support for Families

While the United States has been a leader on equal opportunity in the work place, a 2007 McGill University study found that we are far behind in terms of supporting parents and balancing work and family. In fact, says author Jody Heymann, America ranks "among the worst." In the study of 173 countries, we stood with Liberia, Swaziland, and Papua New Guinea as the only countries providing no paid maternity leave. Of the 169 countries that guarantee paid maternity leave, 98 of them provide 14 or more weeks. Among wealthy countries—except ours—parents are entitled to as much as 47 weeks of paid family leave.

To get an idea of how much other countries invest in family leave, consider the comparatively ungenerous Australian policy: eligible working parents receive payments equal to the federal minimum wage, approximately $543 weekly, for a maximum of eighteen weeks of leave. Under another Australian policy passed earlier, every birth or adoption of a child entitles the parent or parents to a "baby bonus" of approximately $5,000 per child plus other benefits.

Lew Daly, "The Case for Paid Family Leave," Newsweek, *August 3, 2009. www .newsweek.com.*

due to the birth or adoption of a child, their own serious illness, or to care for a family member with a serious illness. . . .

Over the last two years, Workplace Flexibility 2010 at Georgetown Law and the Berkeley Center on Health, Economic & Family Security at UC Berkeley School of Law have collaborated to create this proposal. We followed a careful and lengthy process to reach the conclusions laid out in this report. We looked at the reasons people need paid time off from work for health and caregiving and what happens if they don't get it. We scrutinized how things work right now in the private sector and under current law to understand who has access to paid time off and who doesn't. We carefully constructed our policy response to meet the needs of individuals across income, gender, age, occupation, and industry, while also addressing employer concerns and remaining conscious of financial costs to individuals, employers, and the government.

Because we looked at these issues through a research lens, we can say with confidence that each of the elements we propose as part of FSI is firmly grounded on a foundation from the fields of law, economics and social science. Our proposal recognizes that the 21st century requires a different set of policies than the 20th century. In the 21st century, we need policies designating a national priority to support people who are working—and to help keep them working. We also need policies that spread the costs of paid time off from work for health and caregiving among employers and employees to create a fair and predictable baseline of support.

Below, we outline the rationale for our program design—through our key research findings and our goals and objectives. . . .

The World of Work and Family Has Changed

Profound demographic and societal shifts over the last 40 years have resulted in an increased and acute need for various types of workplace flexibility, including paid time off for health and caregiving reasons. For example:

- In most families, the family-based caregiving safety net in the form of a "stay-at-home spouse" no longer exists. Women are now nearly half of all U.S. workers and are integral to the national economy as primary or co-breadwinners in over two-thirds of households.

- We are living longer, working longer, and providing more care to aging relatives. In fact, caregiving demands are hitting a critical mass. Fifty-nine percent of the 44.4 million caregivers providing care to older individuals are employed, simultaneously juggling work and caregiving responsibilities.

- Health technology has advanced in ways we could never have imagined 50 years ago. Health conditions that previously would have resulted in death or an inability to work now often can be treated through medication, short-term therapies, and surgery, allowing individuals to get back to work within a matter of weeks.

- People with serious illnesses and temporary disabilities now are able to stay in the workforce and are expected to support themselves through work. In fact, with the passage of the Americans with Disabilities Act, these individuals are empowered to work and contribute to the economy.

- The above changes have led to increased levels of reported work-family conflict. Americans want more workplace flexibility. Seventy-six percent of likely voters say they favor extending the current law to provide paid leave. Both men and women experience this tug, and the need for flexibility and paid time off goes beyond one type of family or one type of industry.

Catching up with Societal Changes

Despite the on-the-ground reality facing most Americans, neither the private sector nor public policy has met the demand for paid time off for health and caregiving reasons.

- Working families need paid time off for parental care for a new child, temporary disability, and caregiving reasons, but current access is extremely variable and depends on employer, occupation, income, industry, gender, union membership, and number of hours worked. What's more, there is huge variation in how employers provide paid time-off benefits, including formal insurance, self-insured benefits, informal policies, and PTO (paid time off) banks.

- Disparity continues to exist between women and men regarding who takes time off for caregiving reasons and for bonding with a new child, driven in part by the fact that men continue to earn more than their wives

- The Family and Medical Leave Act (FMLA) provides critical protections, but has two key failings: Its protections reach only about half the workforce, and because the leave is unpaid, many simply cannot afford to take it.

- No federal programs exist to provide paid time off for health and caregiving reasons, and there are only a few state programs that provide income replacement for these reasons.

- Many, many working Americans lack access to paid time off all together—most frequently those who are low-wage and part-time workers.

Supporting Families Has Public Health Benefits

Beyond the sheer need for more work-family support, there are many reasons why income replacement for personal and family health events is good—even critical—for society. . . . The reasons: better outcomes for children, greater gender equity, more secure family incomes, and positive business outcomes. Here we provide a few highlights.

Improved Health and Well-Being for Children and Their Caregivers: Income replacement for new parents has tremendous benefits for the health and well-being of children and their caregivers. Parental leave of 12 weeks or more is correlated with many positive health outcomes for children. Further, parental workplace flexibility during the first year of a child's life, including a significant amount of time off and/or flexibility in scheduling, can have positive developmental and cognitive effects for children.

Parents also benefit from time off to care for newborn, newly adopted, or newly placed foster children. For women, returning early to work, particularly if earlier than preferred, is associated with greater amounts of stress and higher rates of depression. Fathers and non-biological parents (e.g., adoptive or foster parents) also benefit from having time to bond with their children. Although men in the United States rarely take much time off following the birth or adoption of a new child, those who do are more involved in the care of their children later, resulting in stronger long-term, father-child relationships. Time off for foster or adoptive parents is also important because these parents may not have had the same amount of time to prepare psychologically and emotionally for the arrival of the child and are often not present at the birth of the child.

By contrast, returning to work very soon after birth, (i.e., six weeks or less) is associated with a variety of negative outcomes for both parents and children. These include higher rates of infant mortality, lower rates of breastfeeding, lower rates of immunizations and well-baby care, and a higher incidence of maternal physical and mental health concerns.

Greater Income Security: FSI provides greater income security for workers and their families who need time off for a health or caregiving reason. The case for increased income security is especially strong for those events that are unplanned, such as one's own serious illness or the need to provide care for a suddenly seriously ill family member. It is well documented that working caregivers often suffer significant financial hardship.

Better Business Outcomes: Employers stand to gain from the provision of wage replacement for their temporarily disabled workers or for those needing time off to provide care. A worker's faster and more complete recovery, associated with paid time off, reduces the cost of foregone productivity. Employers may also benefit from reduced health care costs since employees will have time off to recover from an illness or injury instead of developing a chronic problem. Providing workers with wage replacement during time off for caregiving is also advantageous to business. Recent research shows that people who receive wage replacement while taking care-related time off are more likely to return to their job following the event and to be more productive overall.

Improved Gender Equity: Women have historically been, and continue to be, primary caregivers in their families, despite the fact that most are now employed outside the home. Women are nearly always the ones who leave the labor force if it is deemed necessary or more cost effective for one parent to do so. Data from other countries that have adopted social insurance programs for paid family leave suggest that providing women with the means to take temporary time off keeps them working and also increases their lifetime wages. Many men would also like to be more involved in caregiving; this is particularly the case among younger generations of workers, who highly value a balance between work and family life. . . .

Our Goals and Objectives

Based on the above research findings, we set out goals and objectives that our ideal program had to meet. Our proposal had to:

- Focus on the primary sources of workplace/workforce conflict regarding the need for time off: personal illness, care for an ill family member, and time off to care for a newborn or newly placed adopted or foster child.
- Provide universal access to paid time off for medical and

caregiving reasons. Universal access means equal access across gender, income, life stage, and industry/occupation.

- Seek to support people who are working and keep them working. Labor force attachment drives many aspects of our program design.

- Ensure efficient delivery of the benefit so that people would get the income replacement simply and when they needed it, not weeks or months later.

- Be budget neutral, spreading the costs among employers and employees rather than increasing the federal deficit.

- Account for employer interests in predictability and administrative ease.

We believe FSI meets all these goals.

Periodical and Internet Sources Bibliography

The following articles have been selected to supplement the diverse views presented in this chapter.

Shelley Waters Boots, Jennifer Ehrle Macomber, and Anna Danziger — "Family Security: Supporting Parents' Employment and Children's Development," *Urban League*, July 16, 2008. www.urban.org.

Piet Bracke, Wendy Christiaens, and Naomi Wauterickx — "The Pivotal Role of Women in Informal Care," *Journal of Family Issues*, vol. 29, no. 10, October, 2008.

Dawn Carlson, Joseph Grzywacz, and Suzanne Zivnuska — "Is Work-Family Balance More than Conflict and Enrichment?," *Human Relations*, vol. 62, Issue 10, October 2009.

Lew Daly — "The Case for Paid Family Leave," *Newsweek*, August 3, 2009.

Giulia El Dardiry and Jody Heymann — "Work and Family Policy in the United States: Past Gaps, Future Possibilities," *International Journal*, vol. 64, 2009.

Melinda Marshall — "Living on the Edge: Families without Health Insurance," *Parenting*, November 2006.

Teri Newton — "Two-Income Trap: Why Many Couples Shouldn't Both Be Working for the Money," *Personal Financial Advice*, May 10, 2007. www.pfadvice.com.

Timothy Noah — "The United States of Inequality," *Slate*, September 3, 2010. www.slate.com.

Lixia Qu — "Supporting Families in Challenging Times," *Family Matters*, vol. 87, no. 6, June 2011.

Joan Williams and Heather Boushey — "The Three Faces of Work-Family Conflict," *Center for American Progress*, January 25, 2010.

OPPOSING
VIEWPOINTS®
SERIES

How Does Lack of Work Affect Families?

Chapter Preface

Concerns about the balance between work and family first really came to the fore in the 1980s as a result of the large-scale entry of women into the workforce. These concerns continued to grow during the 1990s and into the early 2000s, years of general prosperity in the United States and Europe. By the late 2000s however, a deep recession, which affected men particularly hard, forced many to change their viewpoint on work-family balance. Traditional gender roles in particular came in for reassessment, with more men taking the role of stay-at-home parent and more women adopting the role of primary breadwinner.

According to economist Howard J. Wall of the Federal Reserve Bank in Saint Louis, "between the fourth quarter of 2007, when the current recession began, and the first quarter of 2009, men bore 78 percent of the job losses." Looked at another way, for every woman put out of work, 3.4 men lost their jobs. In the popular press, and even on some professional economists' blogs, the term "mancession" was used to describe this phenomenon. As Wall points out, however, in every recession since 1969 men have lost a similar proportion of the jobs; men's employment characteristics—the industries in which they concentrate—just seem to be more susceptible to economic fluctuations.

What was truly unusual in the late 2000s was that while men's overall employment fell, the number of women in the workforce actually rose. Some women lost jobs, but the total number of women seeking—and getting—jobs increased. With more men at home unemployed, and more women out in the workforce, newspapers, magazines, and electronic media began to highlight stories of stay-at-home dads caring for kids, or middle-aged men relying on their wives' income to keep the household afloat. As the recession wore on, however, there was some backlash against the idea that men were bearing the brunt of the country's economic troubles. This reaction also reflected economic realities;

layoffs that hit hardest in male-dominated fields such as construction began to spread to female-dominated fields like healthcare and government services.

It remains to be seen whether the deep recession of the late 2000s, and the relatively weak recovery that followed, will permanently affect employment patterns in the United States. If construction and other "men's" fields pick up in activity, it may be that the traditional male breadwinner role will re-emerge. On the other hand, with women disproportionately employed in what seem to be more stable positions, some couples may just decide that it is too risky to rely on the man's paycheck. The viewpoints that follow debate how households might respond to long lasting economic difficulties.

> "Some 140,000 married men acted as
> their family's primary caregivers last
> year [2008], up from 98,000 in 2003."

High Unemployment Among Men Drives More Women into the Workforce

Alice Gomstyn

The following viewpoint centers on the phenomenon of stay-at-home mothers being prompted to return to the workforce because their husbands have lost jobs. Adjusting to the new situation has been difficult for many of the couples. The men feel a loss of control over their financial situation, while the women regret time not spent with their children. Yet Alice Gomstyn points out that there are bright sides to the situation. Because more women are now primary "breadwinners," the pay gap between men and women may close. Further, in the last few decades women's place in the workforce has been firmly established, so women who now must work outside the home do not face the hostility that women in previous decades might have felt. Gomstyn is a business reporter with ABC News. Her work focuses on consumer issues.

As you read, consider the following questions:

1. How many stay-at-home moms are there in the United States for each stay-at-home dad?
2. On average, how much do women earn for every dollar earned by men?
3. What steps did Brie Hudgins and her family take to help make up for the loss of income caused by her husband's job loss?

While the recession has taken a toll on both sexes, male-dominated industries such as construction and financial services have taken a greater hit than more female-driven professions in areas such as healthcare and education. Between April 2007 and last month [April 2009], the unemployment rate for men age 16 and older more than doubled to 10 percent; among women, the unemployment rate also increased, but less dramatically—from 4.4 percent to 7.6 percent.

A New Economic Reality

For families with children, this new economic reality is bolstering an already-growing trend: wives taking on roles as primary breadwinners while husbands—these days, often newly-unemployed husbands—stay home to become primary caregivers.

"It wasn't what we originally planned, we can't really say for sure how long we want to do this, but it works for us," said Brie Hudgins, 31, an insurance adjuster in Mississippi.

Hudgin's husband, Jeremy, lost his job at a student loan company more than a year ago and now stays home with the couple's two daughters. Jeremy Hudgins says he relishes spending time with his children, but his new role hasn't come without hang-ups, including a hit to his ego and the disapproval of his parents.

"My parents don't really get what I'm doing," he said. "They think I should be out with a job—I explained to them, it's not that easy to get a job right now."

While married stay-at-home mothers outnumber their male counterparts by more than 38 to 1, according to recent U.S. Census bureau statistics, the number of stay-at-home fathers has grown substantially: Some 140,000 married men acted as their family's primary caregivers last year [2008], up from 98,000 in 2003.

Before the recession, job loss wasn't necessarily the key factor driving the increase in stay-at-home dads. Monique Derenia, who spent a year researching and filming California stay-at-home dads for her short documentary, "Why Not Dad?", said she found that many fathers volunteered to stay home.

"Most of them talked about the value in and of itself of being more involved than their fathers were," Derenia said. "When it became clear that they would have this opportunity, they jumped at the chance to be more involved with parenting."

The Pay Gap

The men could afford to stay home with their children, Derenia said, because often their wives earned higher salaries than they did.

But today, wives who assume the roles of primary breadwinners in the face of a husband's job loss may . . . not be as fortunate. According to most recent U.S. Census data, women on average make about 78 cents for each dollar earned by men.

For the Hudgins, it's a statistic that hits home: Her $30,000 salary is about a third lower than what her husband used to earn, she said.

To make ends meet, the couple has spent their savings, dipped into Jeremy Hudgins' 401(k) retirement plan and gotten help from family. While Brie Hudgins has free health insurance through her job and her children receive health insurance through the state, the family can't afford coverage for Jeremy Hudgins.

For Brie Hudgins, worrying about her family's financial straits [is] exhausting.

"When the air conditioner broke two weeks ago, I silently freaked out," she said. "I shuffled money around in my head, thinking how are we going to pay for this."

The 'Great Recession' Has Prompted More Married Women to Return to the Workplace

In a study published this September in the journal *Family Relations*, researchers Marybeth J. Mattingly and Kristin E. Smith of the University of New Hampshire found that wives were more likely to enter the job market or increase their hours when their husbands were out of work between May 2007 and May 2008 than when their husbands were out of work amid prosperity four years earlier. These women were also three times more likely to enter the labor force than women whose husbands were working and 51 percent more likely to increase their hours.

Diane Brady, "More Wives Head for Work," Businessweek, *September 30, 2010.*
www.businessweek.com.

If there's a silver lining to the income challenges faced by today's growing number of breadwinner women, said Andrew Stettner, the deputy director of the National Employment Law Project, it's that they may help increase pressure to shrink the pay gap between men and women.

"We all know of anecdotes [that men] will get a higher starting salary because the boss knows they have to support a family," Stettner said. "Hopefully, that will start reversing."

Respect for Working Women

For now, the good news for women like Hudgins is that they face a lot less adversity than they would have years ago.

The last time that the economic climate moved large numbers of women into primary breadwinner roles was the Great Depression, said Stephanie Coontz, the director of research at the Council on Contemporary Families, a non-profit group at the University of Illinois.

That era came decades before the women's movement that "clearly established women's rights to work" and so working women met with "huge hostility" for supposedly taking jobs away from men, Coontz said.

"The good news in this recession is that families are more grateful and respectful when a woman steps up to the plate that way," Coontz said. "They've already been working, their families respect the work they've been doing, and so as they need to step up to the plate even more it's not such a total shock to the family system."

But the shock hasn't disappeared completely. Jennifer Walden, a Bowling Green, [Kentucky] mother of two says that her new role in controlling the family finances has brought some tension to her marriage.

"He has to ask me if he needs something . . . if we can afford this, we can afford that," said Walden, 39, who works as a forecast analyst for an apparel company and whose husband lost his job in October. "I just make all the decisions because I know what needs to be done and I don't consult with him. That might be bad, but right now it's all I know to do."

Adjusting to New Roles

For his part, Walden's husband Don says he doesn't mind that Jennifer makes the family's financial choices. But he does miss working.

"I've always enjoyed going to work," he said. "I've always wanted to be the man of the house. It was a big adjustment, it really was."

But like Jeremy Hudgins, Don Walden said he too treasures the time he now gets to spend with his children.

"I'm just using this time to bond with my sons. I have a very important job, I think," Don Walden said. "It's not one that pays any money, but it pays in a different way."

As fathers grow accustomed to their roles inside the homes, some new breadwinning moms must contend with being the parent who is now less in tune with their children.

"Now I come home, I'm out off the loop some days. I wasn't there to see Sammy hit her head so I don't know why she was upset. I don't know what Sammy's favorite gummy bears are anymore," said Brie Hudgins. "I'm not the one with them all the time. I'm not the preferred parent anymore."

Jennifer Walden said it's been difficult to explain to her children why they see her so much less than they see their father.

"Little minds just don't understand what's going on in the world," she said. "I tell them I have to go to work so I can make money for more toys."

Still, both women say they value the relationships their children are developing with their fathers.

"I know how important it is for their emotional growth, and it'll be huge when they get older," Brie Hudgens said. "They'll know, no matter what, their daddy adores them."

> *"The myth of the mancession has assumed a staying power beyond what those initial numbers appeared to support: it taps into larger cultural and economic anxieties . . ."*

Anxieties About Changing Gender Roles Fuel the 'Mancession' Myth

Alice O'Connor

The following viewpoint critiques the idea that the economic slow-down of the late 2000s was a "mancession," a recession disproportionately impacting men. Alice O'Connor writes that men may have lost more jobs, but argues that is because male-dominated fields such as construction and finance were hardest hit by the downturn. Further, as the recession progressed, layoffs spread to white-collar and clerical workers, reducing the unemployment gap between men and women. O'Connor believes that the myth of disproportionate male suffering during the economic down turn of the late 2000s enabled society to avoid serious discussion about the changing gender roles in the United States workforce. O'Connor is a professor of history at the University of California, Santa Barbara. Her research and writing focus on poverty and wealth, social and urban policy, and inequality in the United States. She is the author of Social Science for What? Philanthropy and the Social Question in a World Turned Rightside Up.

As you read, consider the following questions:
1. What percentage of construction jobs were held by men?
2. According to the author, the "mancession" narrative is linked to what larger narrative about change in American society?
3. What are two consequences of the "historical fictions" about women's participation in the workforce?

As an analysis, the myth of the "mancession" may have started out as an overly-stylized reading of labor market statistics. Men lost a larger share of jobs than women at the outset of the Great Recession in 2007, according to widely-reported Bureau of Labor Statistics measures tracking trends through spring 2009. This led University of Michigan economist and American Enterprise Institute (AEI) scholar Mark J. Perry to conclude that there was a "historic" and "unprecedented" gender gap in unemployment favoring women by as much as two percentage points—a gap that actually has been closing more recently as cutbacks shift from the male-dominated construction and manufacturing sectors to education, human services, and other areas where women predominate.

Cultural Anxieties

But as an idea, the myth of the mancession has assumed a staying power beyond what those initial numbers appeared to support: it taps into larger cultural and economic anxieties that predate the Great Recession and that have to do with changing relations between men and women. This is revealed nowhere more powerfully than in the late, great passing of the "traditional" two-parent family, in which men could expect to be the chief—if not the solo—breadwinners.

Of course, there is rarely just one way to read statistical measures, and on these grounds alone the "mancession" has been subject to much dispute. More fine-grained analyses of the data, for example, show considerable differences in the impact of male job loss across lines of class, race, age, and region; not all men have been affected equally by the downturn, nor women for that matter, suggesting at the very least that there is more to the so-called gender gap than meets the eye. Nor has the Great Recession shown any "favor" to women when it comes to wage losses and poverty rates, both of which are on the rise. And historical experience reminds us that men have also lost the large majority of jobs in past recessions, as they did in the Great Depression, due to the fact that they are disproportionately represented in traditionally hard-hit and better-paying sectors of the economy. Indeed, one could use this observation to conclude that the gender gap in job loss reveals just how stratified the labor market remains, with nearly 90 percent of construction jobs held by men, and nearly 70 percent in manufacturing. The "mancession," however, comes to a simpler, if misleading conclusion: men suffered far more from the Great Recession than women, and by the time we actually recover, they may find themselves even further behind. As characterized by Perry when he first started writing about the unemployment "gender gap," what women were experiencing as a "downturn" was a "catastrophe" for men.

It is in taking this line that the myth of the "mancession" most clearly links up to a larger narrative that, in its starkest expressions, presents a story of female ascendancy and male decline. Indeed, news reports of the mancession almost invariably come wrapped up in a bundle of statistics suggesting that women are outdoing men in all sorts of other "historic" and "unprecedented" ways, from higher numbers of college and post-graduate degrees to larger shares of consumer spend-

"Your husband is on line two. He says it's an emergency. He wants to know how to work the microwave." Cartoon by Jerry King, wwwCartoonStock.com. Copyright © Jerry King. Reproduction rights obtainable from www.CartoonStock.com.

ing and growing importance, if not yet outright leadership, as breadwinners in the household economy. Men, in the zero-sum logic that underlies the larger narrative, are losing out, not just in terms of relative economic position, but in the sense of authority and, well, *manliness* that once anchored their sense of identity.

Historical Fiction

The fearful, not to mention highly exaggerated, narrative of women's looming economic and cultural dominance is hardly new. By invoking it, the myth of the mancession carries on a long tradition of more deeply rooted historical fictions that for decades were used to diminish or otherwise distort the significance of women's participation in the paid labor force—and to defend the sanctity of the male breadwinner ideal. Until well into the twentieth century, these fictions mostly served as a form of willful ignorance, if not downright denial, treating women as at best temporary, non-essential workers without legitimate aspiration for better-paying, high-skilled jobs, let alone long-term careers. In formulations that still haunt us today, they treated African American and other minority female breadwinning as an expression of cultural pathology, a "matriarchy" that prevented men from taking their rightful roles as household heads. Such fictions persisted despite a similarly long tradition of social investigation documenting the realities—and the necessity—of female employment and household work. And they had real and lasting consequences: in well-documented government policies, union and private sector practices that denied women access to better job opportunities at equal pay; in decades of organized resistance to adequate child care provisions for parents in the paid labor force; in job training, employment, and social welfare programs that consistently favored male over female earnings capacity; and in a whole host of economic practices and cultural cues that sent women "back" to more traditionally subordinate positions in the wake of the unprecedented job opportunities that had been opened up by World War II.

The myth of the mancession may not take us back to the dark days of cultural denial, but its exaggerated claims echo the old stereotype-laden, zero-sum ways of thinking that pit the fortunes of female earners against those of men. In recent months, it has stirred a minor skirmish in the ongoing culture wars between feminists and the right. Echoing the idea that men were the chief victims of the Great Recession, AEI resident scholar and author of "The War Against Boys" Christina Hoff Sommers accused feminists of "skewing" President Obama's initial stimulus plan by insisting on equal treatment for women, who in "mancession" logic did not need the jobs as much as men. Writing more recently on the AEI blog, Mark Perry similarly criticized the Obama National Economic Council for issuing its report on "Jobs and Economic Security for America's Women" in the midst of what he now refers to as the "Great Mancession", calling it "one-sided and misguided" to focus on women, when they are doing "so much better than men."

If history is any guide, perpetuating the myth of the mancession could very well exact a price: not only in thwarting long overdue discussions of a jobs agenda that is fair and equitable across the board, but in preventing a more frank coming to terms with the cultural anxieties—and politics—that prevent us from articulating, and embracing, a more realistic, equitable, and genuinely shared breadwinner ideal. Given the challenges ahead, that's a reckoning we can't afford to put off.

> *"Men have borne the brunt of job reductions because male-dominated industries are facing the severest contractions . . ."*

Recession Leads Men to Rethink Their Traditional Breadwinner Role

Catherine Holahan

According to the following viewpoint, the "Great Recession" impacted men's employment more than that of women, but there may be a silver lining. Journalist Catherine Holahan's interviews with several unemployed young men indicate that they look at the involuntary time out of the workforce as an opportunity to explore other fields. Because there is a much larger number of women in the workforce than in previous eras of high unemployment, many men have the safety net of an additional income in the household. At the same time, married men still feel some pressure to fulfill the traditional breadwinner role, while single men are worried that they will appear to be financially unstable to potential partners. Holahan, a graduate of Princeton University, is a reporter for Businessweek *specializing in technology.*

As you read, consider the following questions:

1. What was the suicide rate during the Great Depression and what does a comparison with the current rate indicate about how men are reacting to unemployment?
2. What percentage of current households have two wage-earners?
3. What sector of the economy, highlighted in the article, continued hiring despite the recession of the late 2000s?

There's a gender gap in this recession, and this time men are on the losing side of it.

The unemployment rate for men is nearly 2 full percentage points higher, at 8.8% [as of April, 2009], than the rate for women. Before the recession, the jobless rate was virtually the same for both genders: 4.5% for men and 4.6% for women in November 2007.

But now, more than two-thirds of those looking for full-time work are men, according to the U.S. Department of Labor. Nearly 70% of the extended layoffs in the final quarter of 2008 affected men.

Men have borne the brunt of job reductions because male-dominated industries are facing the severest contractions, according to the Labor Department.

- Construction: One in five workers in this field is unemployed, and more than 95% of those out of work are men, according to the department's March employment report.
- Manufacturing: That same data show that manufacturing jobs—of which nearly 80% are held by men—declined 4.5% from the fourth quarter of 2008 to the first quarter of this year.
- Finance: The largely male financial industry cut 260,110 jobs in 2008, according to outplacement firm Challenger, Gray & Christmas.

And there are few signs that these industries are done shrinking: Just last week [in April, 2009], banking giant UBS said it would lay off 500 financial advisers.

Meanwhile, industries with predominantly female work forces, such as health care and education, are growing. While nearly every other major industry was laying off workers, education and health services actually added about 8,000 jobs in February and March.

Comparison with the Depression Era

The last time the U.S. dealt with such a large gender gap in unemployment was during the Great Depression. During that time, suicide rates for men hit an all-time high, as many unemployed men felt their sense of purpose and identity undermined by their inability to fulfill their traditional provider role. The suicide rate peaked at 17 per 100,000 population during the Depression. It is now around 11 per 100,000 and hasn't increased in recent years.

But there's reason to believe that men have become much more resilient about job losses. In the 70 years since the Depression, the male identity has become less tied to that of sole family provider. That's partly due to the large number of women who help support their families. More than 40% of households now have two wage-earners.

"The idea of being a provider is the bedrock experience of American masculinity . . . but the fact that most of these men are in two-career couples will mute some of the possible depressing elements of their unemployment," says Michael Kimmel, an author and sociologist at New York state's Stony Brook University.

Changing attitudes toward family life and employment are also mitigating the disappointment associated with a job loss. Whereas before identity was closely tied to career or a role in the home, Kimmel says, now both men and women have a broader idea of what defines them. Jobs, family roles, hobbies and talents all now contribute to self-identity.

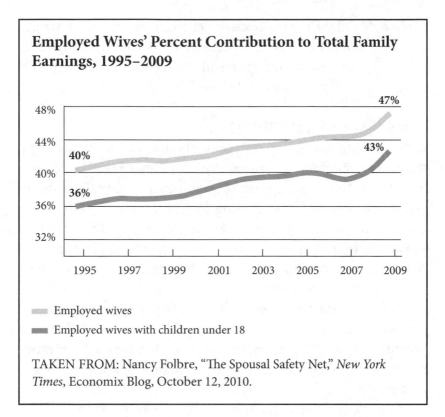

Employed Wives' Percent Contribution to Total Family Earnings, 1995–2009

Legend:
- Employed wives
- Employed wives with children under 18

TAKEN FROM: Nancy Folbre, "The Spousal Safety Net," *New York Times*, Economix Blog, October 12, 2010.

The day Bjorn Eriksen was laid off, he went straight to a bar. A portfolio manager for Washington Mutual, Eriksen saw the cuts coming long before the official announcement in January. Still, the warning didn't erase the shock of actually receiving the news. Eriksen, 27, hadn't lost just a high-powered banking job. He had lost everything that went along with it: the influence, the status, the salary.

But Eriksen didn't go to the pub to wallow in self-pity or shame. He went to talk about his newfound joblessness with other unemployed friends and former co-workers. A few days later, he found himself hanging out in a Seattle coffee shop, again chatting with other unemployed guys about their situations.

"I think some of the stigma is gone," says Eriksen, who admits he was initially concerned that he would be viewed as a guy who couldn't take care of himself, let alone provide for a family or take a woman out to someplace nice. "If you meet someone who is unemployed, you have something to immediately talk about. . . . It's almost like a little club."

Dead End or Opportunity?

For some men, unemployment presents an opportunity to escape the rat race and find something more fulfilling. Sean Harvey, the founder of New York career consultancy Boerum Consulting, says more men are now coming to him looking for jobs that have a better work-life balance. Many, he says, feel that they had worked long, hard hours only to be unceremoniously laid off. Now they want positions that allow them to focus more on their homes, families and hobbies.

"Folks are starting to say, 'I have been giving so much to my job, and look how I have been treated,'" Harvey says. "Many are saying, 'I want to try entrepreneurial roles where I have more control or go to companies that are going to walk the talk when it comes to work-life balance.'"

Eriksen can relate. He is no longer looking for jobs in the financial industry. After a few months of reflecting on his time at Washington Mutual, Eriksen says he realized he never liked banking all that much. What drew him to the industry was its seeming stability and that it paid more than enough to support his wife and start a family. Now, his priorities have changed. That's partly due to Eriksen's split from his wife before he was laid off and partly due to his desire to have work he's passionate about.

"I'd like to have a complete career shift doing something almost entirely unrelated to finance," Eriksen says. "I was in the music industry and marketing before, so that is what I would like to get back into."

The desire to find personally meaningful work is leading many men to the nonprofit sector, Harvey says. It's also an area that's hiring. About 77,000 senior management positions were open at nonprofits in 2008, according to Bridgespan Group, a nonprofit advisory firm in Boston.

Bryan Munson is considering nonprofit jobs. In February, the New Jersey resident was laid off from a news and marketing position at Loud.com, an online social-networking company financed in part by Universal Music Group. At first, he was in shock. Munson, now 27, was in college during the recession of 2001. He was still operating under the assumption that long hours and hard work guaranteed job security, no matter what the economic circumstances.

"I was working from home, and they called me up and said, 'Hey, you don't have a job anymore. . . . We have to cut back,'" says Munson, who added that he had often worked 15-hour days. "I was thinking, 'How could they do that?'"

Breadwinner Idea Gets Stale

Munson says he would like to continue to work with music, but he's open to anything that makes him feel good about his employment at the end of the day. He says he won't be picky for long. Though he doesn't feel embarrassed about getting laid off, he still feels a duty to take care of his live-in girlfriend, who has been unemployed since leaving a job to join him in New Jersey.

"I owe it to her to give her certain things," says Munson, adding that while his girlfriend is not pressuring him to support her, he feels responsible for providing financially. "We are not engaged now, but we will be one day, and I want to provide for her. The question is how?"

The length of unemployment will be key in determining just how much psychological damage this recession will inflict. Though many men remain upbeat about what they see as a temporary setback, that could change as weeks of unemployment stretch into months. That may be particularly true for men who still identify with being a breadwinner, author-sociologist Kimmel says.

Kyle Sullivan, a 32-year-old producer in New Jersey who recently lost his job at a small media-distribution company, says single men are under pressure to always be employed. Though opinions on unemployment may have relaxed in recent months, given rising rates, he thinks many women still assume that an unemployed guy must be lazy or otherwise unfit.

Sullivan began looking for a job within hours of hearing that his company was downsizing. To him, being unemployed for four months would be absolutely unacceptable, even though he has enough savings to continue to pay his bills.

"You want to be able to take a person out on a date or go to the movies and pay for it. You don't want the girl to have to pay for it," says Sullivan. "You don't want to be that guy."

| "Rather than opting out of the labor force, mothers increased their labor force participation over the recession."

Women Face Unique Challenges in the Poor Economy

United States Congress Joint Economic Committee

The following viewpoint, excerpted from a report by the United States Congress Joint Economic Committee, describes the situation of women, particularly mothers, during the "Great Recession" of the late 2000s. Much popular analysis has focused on the loss of jobs among men during the economic slowdown of the late 2000s. This viewpoint shows, however, that women have experienced a higher proportion of job loss in the 2000s downturn than in previous recessions. For example, in the recession of the early 1990s, women only lost two jobs for every hundred jobs lost by men. In the late 2000s, that ratio had risen to forty-six for every hundred. While men still lost more jobs, women were harder hit than their female predecessors in earlier recessions. And women face additional challenges in hard economic times. Those who share households with newly unemployed men are often forced

United States Congress Joint Economic Committee, "Working Mothers in the Great Recession," United States Senate, May 10, 2010.

to take low paying, part-time work to make ends meet. Single women are even worse off; with no potential second earner in the household, layoffs or wage reductions could mean disaster. The Joint Economic Committee is a bipartisan body of the United States Congress, made up of members of both the House and Senate. Its staff prepared the report from which this viewpoint is taken.

As you read, consider the following questions:

1. How much did the share of unemployed mothers increase from 2007 to 2009?
2. In 2009 what proportion of working mothers were the sole jobholder in their family, and how many sole earner working moms did this mean in absolute numbers?
3. In 2007 in what percentage of married-couple families was the mother the sole jobholder? In 2009?

The Great Recession has taken a huge toll on working families. The vast majority of jobs lost were lost by men, but a substantial number of jobs were lost by women during this recession. From December 2007 to April 2010, women lost 46 jobs for every 100 jobs lost by men. By comparison, during the 2001 recession, women lost 17 jobs for every 100 lost by men and women lost less than 2 jobs for every 100 jobs lost by men during the 1990s recession. Indeed, in recent months, women lost jobs while men gained jobs. From October 2009 to March 2010, women lost 22,000 jobs while men gained 260,000. Women's increased vulnerability to the business cycle has important repercussions for families' economic security. This report provides an updated look at the employment situation of working mothers with children under 18 years old, and examines the impact of the recession on their participation in the labor market using unpublished data from the Bureau of Labor Statistics.

More Families Depend on Working Mothers

Over the past several decades, women have played a role of growing importance in the labor force. It is clear that in the wake of the Great Recession, families continue to rely upon mothers' employment. Rather than opting out of the labor force, mothers increased their labor force participation over the recession. The share of mothers working or actively searching for work increased from 71.0 percent to 71.4 percent between 2007 and 2009.

During that time, mothers' participation shifted away from full-time work to unemployment and part-time work, with the share of all mothers working full-time dropping to 48.3 percent in 2009 from 51.3 percent in 2007. The share of all mothers working part-time rose almost a full percentage point to 17.2 percent, while the share of unemployed mothers increased 2.6 percentage points to 5.9 percent.

Of the 21.7 million mothers who were usually employed in 2009, two-thirds were in a dual-earner family. But the remaining one-third—7.5 million mothers—were the sole job-holders in their family, either because their spouse was unemployed or out of the labor force, or because they were heads of household.

Until recently, job losses were concentrated in male-dominated industries like construction and manufacturing, so fathers were more likely to lose a job and mothers were more likely to hold onto their employment or quickly find a new job. As job losses slowed in the final months of 2009, women continued to lose jobs as men found employment.

In order to cope with the widespread job losses during the recession, many parents who were previously out of the labor force entered the workforce, presumably to compensate for a spouse's lost wages. In general, mothers are far more likely than fathers to be out of the labor force, thus the movement of parents into the labor market largely reflects that of mothers. In 2007, 35.2 percent of two-parent families had only one employed parent, compared to 36.8 percent in 2009. That 1.6 percentage point net difference masks more dramatic changes in the share of families solely dependent on a *mother's* earnings. In fact, families where the mother was the only jobholder rose 2.5 percentage points from 4.9 percent of married-couple families to 7.4 percent. More than ever, families depend on mothers' work.

Many married mothers who looked for employment in order to bolster their families' economic security found it difficult to find work because of the severe shortage of jobs. The labor force participation rate rose for married mothers between 2007 and 2009, meaning that more married mothers were searching for a job. However, the employment-to-population ratio—the so called 'employment rate'—fell over the recession from 66.7 percent to 65.5 percent, indicating that fewer married mothers actually had a job. The unemployment rate nearly doubled to 5.8 percent during that time—a clear sign that mothers wanting work struggled to find a job.

High Unemployment Among Single Mothers

Families headed by single mothers had no second parent to fall back on in the face of job loss or reduced hours and earnings. Labor force participation was already higher among these women, with over three-quarters (76.5 percent) of women maintaining families working or actively searching for work in 2007. Consequently, the recession did not boost their participation rate. Instead, the participation rate of mothers maintaining families dropped to 75.8 percent indicating that many single mothers dropped out of the labor force probably because they were unable to find work.

For single mothers in the labor force, unemployment increased dramatically during the recession. Between 2007 and 2009, the unemployment rate of single mothers increased from 8.0 percent to 13.6 percent. Single mothers of children under the age of 6 who are not yet in school had an unemployment rate of 17.5 percent in 2009. For these mothers, even searching for work can be a challenge because they may have to find child care in order to go on an interview, and high costs of child care eat away a substantial chunk of their earnings once they do find a job.

Many women have been unable to find full-time employment because of the weak labor market. In 2009, 3.3 million women worked part-time for economic reasons, meaning that either their hours had been cut back or that they searched for full-time work but could only [find] a part-time job. Some of those part-time workers usually worked part-time but would have preferred to move to full-time work, likely because of economic hardship such as a spouse's job loss.

Mothers Face a Part-Time Penalty

Part-time workers face a severe earnings penalty, with a wage equal to as little as 60 percent of the wage for full-time workers in the same occupation. Part-time work also means lower earnings over time, and part-time jobs usually do not come with the same health benefits, paid time-off for vacation and sick leave, or pension benefits that full-time workers receive.

Over one-third (35 percent, or 6.2 million) of all women working part-time in 2009 were mothers. For many of those, including 2.7 million mothers with children less than 6 years old and not yet in school, working a part-time job also means finding part-time child care. The part-time earnings penalty is even more devastating for those mothers because part-time child care can be just as costly as full-time care.

Families depend on women's earnings. Mothers' work is vital not only for their families' economic security, but also for the strength of the American economy as a whole. Understanding and addressing the impact of the Great Recession on mothers is a crucial piece of the economic recovery.

Periodical and Internet Sources Bibliography

The following articles have been selected to supplement the diverse views presented in this chapter.

Valerie Adrian and Stephanie Coontz
"The Long-Range Impact of the Recession on Families," Augusta, Maine: Council on Contemporary Families, 2010. www.contemporaryfamilies.org.

Emily Bazelon
"When Men Lose Their Jobs," *Slate*, March 12, 2009. www.slate.com.

Diane Brady
"More Wives Head for Work," *Businessweek*, September 30, 2010. www.businessweek.com.

Congressional Joint Economic Committee Staff
"Women in the Recession," Washington, DC: United States Senate, 2009. jec.senate.gov.

Kathleen Deveny
"Families Need to Man up— the Recession's Silver Lining," *Newsweek*, December 14, 2009.

Elisabeth Eaves
"In This Recession, Men Drop Out," *Forbes.com*, April 10, 2009. www.forbes.com.

Zachary Karabell
"We Are Not in This Together— Young, Minority Men Who Didn't Earn Much to Begin with Are Hit Hardest by Unemployment," *Newsweek*, April 20, 2009.

Rick Martin and Tony Dokoupil
"Can Manhood Survive the Recession?" *Newsweek*, April 17, 2011.

Don Peck
"How a New Jobless Era Will Transform America," *The Atlantic*, March, 2010. www.theatlantic.com.

Mark Roth
"Recession Has Taken Hidden Toll on Black Families," *Post-Gazette*, June 7, 2011. www.post-gazette.com.

Judith Warner
"What the Great Recession Has Done to Family Life," *New York Times*, August 6, 2010. www.nytimes.com.

For Further Discussion

Chapter 1

1. What evidence does Pamela Stone present to make her case that husbands pressure women to give up their careers? Are her sources biased and if so, why? What additional information might have made her case stronger?

2. According to Moe and Shandy, how do women who have left the workforce counteract the stigma associated with that decision? What indications do the authors present that the women actually feel this stigma? Can you offer an alternative explanation of the women's activities (e.g., volunteering) that didn't involve a need to combat stigma?

Chapter 2

1. Why might the "time-budget diary" method of investigating people's hours spent on housework or childcare, used in the Margaret O'Brien article, be inaccurate? Can you think of more accurate methods?

2. The article by Daly, Ashbourne, and Hawkins is based on qualitative research. What do you think is meant by qualitative research and how might it differ from quantitative research like that presented in the first viewpoint of Chapter 2 (O'Brien)? What are some advantages and disadvantages of each approach?

Chapter 3

1. Why do Boushey and Williams believe that politicians who support family-leave policies will be rewarded by voters at the polls? What evidence do they use to support their position? Is their case based solely on empirical data (surveys, past elections) or are their elements of speculation involved?

2. Do you believe that Lotte Bailyn's use of two case studies of companies with flexible work rules presents sufficient evidence that such rules will be effective in all companies? How might the type of business affect how workplace flexibility will fit with a company's core activities? How might Bailyn's study be improved?

Chapter 4

1. What are the key points in O'Connor's case that the "mancession" was largely a myth? Is her explanation for the "mancession" idea's popularity supported by empirical evidence? If so, what is that evidence and if not, how does she build her case?

2. In Stephanie Hanes's article, which men seem most comfortable with their new role as a stay-at-home dad? Do you think the picture that Hanes's presents, based on a small number of couples, reflects the general ability of men to adjust to changing roles in marriage? Why or why not?

3. According to Catherine Holahan, what is a positive outcome of unemployment among young men? Is her argument supported by the number of interviews she reports on? Why or why not?

Organizations to Contact

The editors have compiled the following list of organizations concerned with the issues debated in this book. The descriptions are derived from materials provided by the organizations. All have publications or information available for interested readers. The list was compiled on the date of publication of the present volume; names, addresses, phone and fax numbers, and e-mail and Internet addresses may change. Be aware that many organizations take several weeks or longer to respond to inquiries, so allow as much time as possible.

Brookings Institute
1775 Massachusetts Ave, NW
Washington, DC 20036
(202) 797-6000
website: www.brookings.edu

The Brookings Institute is one of America's oldest think tanks. Originally associated with the Robert Brookings Graduate School of Economics and government, it is now an independent research and publication organization. It publishes the Brookings Bulletin four times a year as well as Brookings Papers on Economic Activity. One of Brookings's projects is the Center on Children and Families, which "studies policies on the well-being of America's children and their parents, especially children in less-advantaged families." Works published by Brookings on work-life balance include *Reconciling Work and Family Responsibilities*, by Catherine Hein.

Cato Institute
1000 Massachusetts Avenue
Washington, DC 20001-5403
(202) 842-0200 fax: • (202) 842-3490
website: www.cato.org

A libertarian think-tank, the Cato Institute promotes the benefits of the free market and limited government. The Center takes a dim view of government interference with the economy of any kind. This includes involvement in work-family issues. For example, Cato has published, "The Advancing Nanny State: Why the Government Should Stay Out of Child Care" and "The Argument Against Paid Family Leave," both of which oppose government mandates for family leave benefits. These and similar publications are available at Cato's website.

Clearinghouse on International Developments in Child, Youth and Family Policies at Columbia University

1255 Amsterdam Avenue
School of Social Work, Mail Code 4600
New York, NY 10027
(212) 851-2272 • fax: (212) 851-2275
e-mail: childpolicyintl@columbia.edu
website: www.childpolicyintl.org

Columbia University's Clearinghouse on International Developments in Child, Youth and Family Policies provides cross-national, comparative information about the policies affecting children and families in twenty-three advanced industrialized countries. The Clearinghouse website links to detailed reports on countries such as France and Sweden as well as briefer "country profiles" on developing countries such as Thailand and Malaysia. There are also "Issue Briefs," which contain more activist-oriented content—these advocate specific policies and programs to help families around the world.

Corporate Voices for Working Families

1020 19th Street, NW, Suite 750
Washington, DC 20036
(202) 467-8130 • fax: (202) 467-8140
e-mail: lkearney@corporatevoices.org
website: www.cvworkingfamilies.org

Corporate Voices for Working Families is a business lobbying group that seeks to influence the national conversation on public and corporate policy issues involving working families. The nonprofit, nonpartisan organization generally favors private, market-based solutions to work and family balance problems. For example, it promotes increasing the amount that employees themselves can save, tax-free, in Dependent Care Flexible Spending Accounts. The group's publications present business-oriented views on the major issues in the work-family conversation. Some examples include the articles "Corporate Voices Urges Support for Working Families" and "Workplace Flexibility Recommendations." Transcripts of congressional testimony by Corporate Voices's officers are also available at the group's website.

The Institute for Women's Policy Research

1200 18th Street NW, Suite 301
Washington, DC 20036
(202) 785-5100 • fax: (202) 833-4362
e-mail: iwpr@iwpr.org
website: www.iwpr.org

The Institute for Women's Policy Research (IWPR) focuses on issues affecting women. In fact, it claims to be "the leading think tank in the United States focusing primarily on domestic women's issues." Of particular interest to students and researchers involved with work and family issues is IWPR's initiative regarding family leave and sick pay, which has provided the framework for publishing reports such as "Maternity, Paternity, and Adoption Leave in the United States" and "Paid Sick Day Access Rates by Gender and Race/Ethnicity, 2010." These and other similar publications are available for free download at the website.

National Center on Fathers and Families University of Pennsylvania

3440 Market Street, Suite 450

Philadelphia, PA 19104-3325
(215) 573-5500
website: www.ncoff.gse.upenn.edu

The National Center on Fathers and Families is primarily an academic research organization, seeking to advance knowledge of the dynamics of fathers' roles within families. The Center's goal is to produce policy relevant research in areas that have been overlooked and understudied. Its website has a link to a summary of the group's "core learnings" as well as access to a blog and research papers by its individual researchers.

Alfred P. Sloan Foundation

630 Fifth Avenue, Suite 2550
New York, NY 10111
(212) 649-1649 • fax: (212) 757-5117
website: www.sloan.org

The Sloan Foundation is a major source of funding for research and policy initiatives in a wide variety of areas. Of particular interest to those seeking information on work and family balance issues are the foundation's program on "Workplace, Work Force and Working Families" and the related "National Workplace Flexibility Initiative." Started in 2003, the initiative's purpose is "to shape workplace flexibility as a compelling national issue—providing an essential step toward the long-term goal of making workplace flexibility the standard way of working in America." In pursuit of this goal, the foundation sponsored a major conference on workplace flexibility in 2010. Research papers and other materials from the conference can be found at www.workplaceflexibility.org.

Work, Family, and Health Network Kaiser Permanente Center for Health Research

3800 N Interstate Ave.
Portland, OR 97227

(503) 335-6612
e-mail: workfamily@kpchr.org
website: www.kpchr.org/workfamilyhealthnetwork

The Work, Family, and Health Network, hosted by the Kaiser Permanente Center for Health Research, facilitates scientific study of the relationship between workplace stress, family obligations, and worker health. Started in 2005 with funding from the National Institutes of Health and the Centers for Disease Control, the Network has supported researchers at various universities, helping them to conduct studies and disseminate their findings to the wider public. The network's website features links to studies carried out under its auspices.

Bibliography of Books

Willem Adema and
Peter Whiteford

Babies and Bosses: Reconciling Work and Family Life—A Synthesis of Findings for OECD Countries, Paris, France: Organization for Economic Cooperation and Development, 2007.

Jill Duerr Berrick
and Bruce Fuller

Good Parents or Good Workers?: How Policy Shapes Families' Daily Lives, New York: Palgrave Macmillan, 2005.

Alice K. Butterfield,
Cynthia J. Rocha,
and William H.
Butterfield

The Dynamics of Family Policy, Chicago: Lyceum Books, 2010.

Kathleen
Christensen and
Barbara L. Schneider
(eds)

Workplace Flexibility: Realigning 20th-Century Jobs for a 21st-Century Workforce, Ithaca: ILR Press, 2010.

Ann C. Crouter and
Alan Booth

Work-Life Policies, Washington, DC: Urban Institute Press, 2009.

Lara Descartes

Media and Middle Class Moms: Images and Realities of Work and Family, New York: Routledge, 2009.

Marlese Durr and
Shirley A. Hill

Race, Work, and Family in the Lives of African Americans, Lanham, MD: Rowman & Littlefield, 2006.

Kathleen Gerson — *The Unfinished Revolution: How a New Generation Is Reshaping Family, Work, and Gender in America*, New York: Oxford University Press, 2006.

Neil Gilbert — *A Mother's Work: How Feminism, the Market, and Policy Shape Family Life*, New Haven: Yale University Press, 2008.

Jacqueline Goodman-Draper — *Global Perspectives on Gender and Work: Readings and Interpretations*, Lanham, MD: Rowman & Littlefield, 2010.

Diane F. Halpern and Susan E. Murphy — *From Work-Family Balance to Work-Family Interaction: Changing the Metaphor*, Mahwah, NJ: Lawrence Erlbaum, 2005.

Catherine Hein — *Reconciling Work and Family Responsibilities: Practical Ideas from Global Experience*, Geneva: International Labour Office, 2005.

Jerry A. Jacobs and Kathleen Gerson — *The Time Divide: Work, Family, and Gender Inequality*, Cambridge: Harvard University Press, 2006.

Sylvia Lafair — *Don't Bring It to Work: Breaking the Family Patterns That Limit Success*, San Francisco: Jossey-Bass, 2009.

Amy Marcus-Newhall, Diane F. Halpern, and Sherylle J. Tan	*The Changing Realities of Work and Family: A Multidisciplinary Approach*, Malden, MA: Wiley-Blackwell, 2008.
Michele Antoinette Paludi and Presha E. Neidermeyer	*Work, Life, and Family Imbalance: How to Level the Playing Field*, Westport, CT: Praeger, 2007.
Toby L. Parcel and Daniel B. Cornfield	*Work & Family: Research Informing Policy*, Thousand Oaks, CA: Sage Publications, 2000.
Don Peck	*Pinched: How the Great Recession Has Narrowed Our Futures and What We Can Do About It*, New York: Crown Publishing, 2011.
Becky Pettit and Jennifer Lynn Hook	*Gendered Tradeoffs: Family, Social Policy, and Economic Inequality in Twenty-One Countries*, New York: Russell Sage Foundation, 2009.
Steven A.Y. Poelmans and Paula Caligiuri	*Harmonizing Work, Family, and Personal Life: From Policy to Practice*, New York: Cambridge University Press, 2008.
Elizabeth Rudd	*The Changing Landscape of Work and Family in the American Middle Class: Reports from the Field*, Lanham, MD: Lexington Books, 2008.
Leslie Stebbins	*Work and Family in America: A Reference Handbook*, Santa Barbara, CA: ABC-CLIO, 2001.

Patricia Voydanoff — *Work, Family, and Community: Exploring Interconnections*, Mahwah, NJ: Lawrence Erlbaum, 2007.

Christopher Warhurst, Doris Ruth Eikhof, and Axel Haunschild — *Work Less, Live More?: Critical Analysis of the Work-Life Boundary*, NY: Palgrave Macmillan, 2008.

Steven Wisensale — *Family Leave Policy: The Political Economy of Work and Family in America*, Armonk, NY: M.E. Sharpe, 2001.

Hirokazu Yoshikawa, Thomas S. Weisner, and Edward D. Lowe — *Making It Work: Low-Wage Employment, Family Life, and Child Development*, New York: Russell Sage Foundation, 2006.

Index